Christmas '89

To Grandma.
With Love from. Kathy, Andrew.
Rebecca, Joanna Emma

A Country House Companion

TO JOHN HARRIS

Best of Country House Companions

By the same author:

Victorian Pubs

Sweetness and Light: The 'Queen Anne'
Movement 1860–1900

Life in the English Country House: A Social and
Architectural History

Historic Houses of Britain

The Victorian Country House

The Return to Camelot: Chivalry and the English
Gentleman

Alfred Waterhouse and the Natural History
Museum

Robert Smythson: The Elizabethan Country
House

Cities and People: A Social and Architectural
History

Endpapers: The household of Sir John Boileau at
Ketteringham Hall, Norfolk, *c.*1850. The Gothic hall on the
left was built in 1840 for 'hospitalities'.

½ title page: Madame Baccelli's servants at Knole, Kent.
From the painting, *c.*1780 by Almand.

Title page: Mr and Mrs Sperling, of Dynes Hall, Essex, taking
tea together. Diana Sperling, *c.*1815–20.

MARK GIROUARD

A COUNTRY HOUSE COMPANION

CENTURY

LONDON   MELBOURNE   AUCKLAND   JOHANNESBURG

Jacket illustration: A Cricket Match at Canford Manor, Dorset. Viscount Wimborne.

First published in 1987 by Century Hutchinson Ltd., Brookmount House, 62–65 Chandos Place, Covent Garden, London WC2N 4NW

Century Hutchinson Australia Pty Ltd
PO Box 496
16–22 Church Street
Hawthorn
Victoria 3122
Australia

Century Hutchinson New Zealand Limited
PO Box 40–086
Glenfield
Auckland 10
New Zealand

Century Hutchinson South Africa Pty Ltd
PO Box 337
Bergvlei
2012 South Africa

Set by Tradespools Ltd

Printed and bound in Great Britain by Butler and Tanner Ltd, Frome

Designed by Dorothy Girouard

British Library Cataloguing in Publication Data

A Country House companion
   1. Country Homes – England – History
   2. England – Social life and customs
   I. Girouard, Mark
   942'.00880621   DA115

   ISBN 0-7126-1654-3

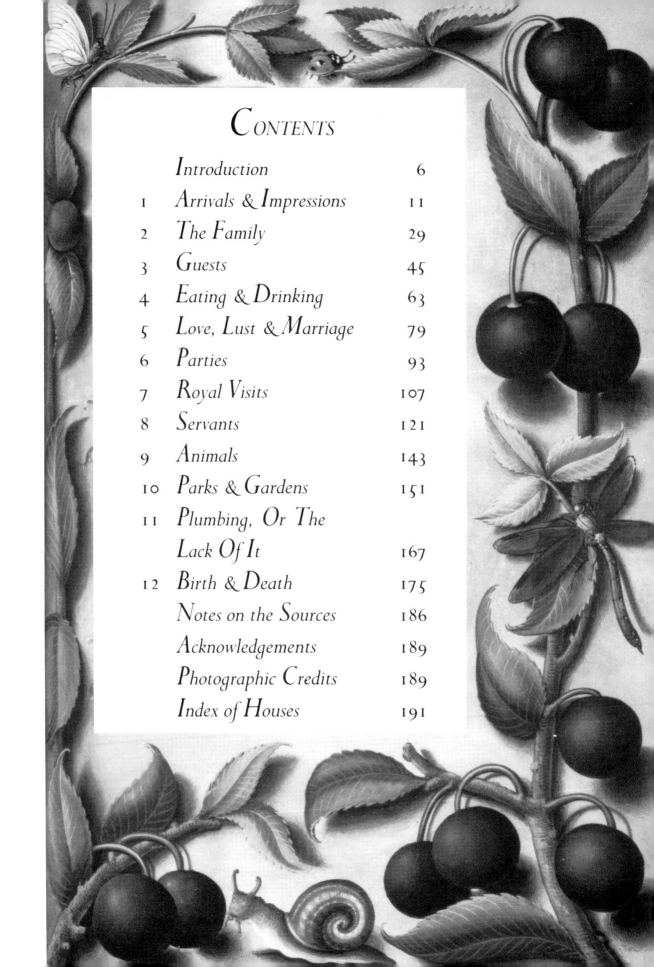

CONTENTS

INTRODUCTION

Anthologies are designed to instruct and to entertain, and tend to lean one way rather than the other. Mine is angled firmly in the direction of entertainment, although I hope that those who are entertained may pick up a little instruction by the way. I have tried to put it together like a menu, or series of menus, contrasting period with period and attitude with attitude, breaking up the main course with appetizers, and setting one savour against another.

In general, my aim has been to take the reader into country houses as an invisible tourist, and allow him or her to see them through the eyes of the people who lived in or visited them, to look over their shoulders as they write, to peer through windows into rooms as they were furnished many hundred years ago, to attend parties, watch dramas unfold, look down dinner tables, or overhear the gossip and grumbles in the servants' hall.

Our knowledge of English country houses, and of the life lived in them, derives from a mass of different sources, apart from the first and basic one, the evidence of the fabric and contents of the houses themselves. But these only tell a limited story, unless other sources are used to illuminate them. Bills, letters, account books, diaries, household regulations, inventories, newspaper reports, descriptions of country houses and poems about them, all add piece by piece and little by little to our knowledge of the way houses were built and why they were built, of the people who lived in them and how they lived in them.

Added to these is the visual evidence of plans, architects' drawings, old photographs, and paintings and drawings of all kinds, from views and conversation pieces commissioned from professional artists to sketches made by children or amateurs. Much of this evidence can still be found in the country houses themselves,

hanging on their walls, pasted in their visitors' books and photo-graph albums, or preserved in their muniment rooms. Much has found its way into public collections. Much has been published, but often in obscure or inaccessible publications. Much still remains unpublished or in manuscript.

I have collected what I find entertaining, unusual or instructive from all kinds of different places, and grouped them together under twelve heads, to give the anthology a little shape. In general, each section is arranged chronologically, but I have not hesitated to go out of the general chronological sequence when I want to illustrate different reactions to one house over the centuries. I have tried to avoid quotations and illustrations which featured in my *Life in the English Country House*. Sometimes, however, I have included a full, or fuller version, of passages which were quoted there only in part. A few of the entries seemed to need elucidation, which I have added either before the entries themselves, or in the introductions to each section. The index at the end gives the location of houses referred to, when this is not given in the text, and an appendix gives the source for each entry in detail. Spelling has been modernized throughout.

The thousands of pieces of evidence out of which an overall picture of the country house can be constructed are like the bits and pieces in a kaleidoscope. Shake them up and a new pattern emerges. Although the patterns may be quite different from one another in the impression they give even of the same house, they are not necessarily misleading or untrue.

One shake of the kaleidoscope, and country houses seem like visions in a dream: visions bathed in sunlight, melting in the mist, or gleaming under the moon. The architecture is frozen, the trees cast long shadows, the houses hover at the end of golden glades, the fruit hangs heavy and abundant in the orchards, the flowers along the garden walks rise in spires drenched and gleaming with dew. This dream-like quality has been felt and described by some of the authors in this anthology – by Marvell in the garden at Appleton House, for instance, by William Howett in the still forecourt of Wootton Lodge, by Henry James looking out from the window at Wroxton Abbey and seeing 'the great soft billows of the lawn melt away into the park'.

Another shake, and another pattern emerges; a pattern of happi-ness, a memory or picture of country houses as places where life is good. It infuses Ben Jonson's poem on Penshurst, with a strength that must reflect a personal reaction by the poet, and not just a desire to please a powerful patron. It is present in Katherine Mansfield's description of Garsington, of 'long conversations between people wandering up and down in the moonlight'. Perhaps it tends to come more often in the form of far-off memories tinged by nostalgia, but none the less vivid, like Constance Sitwell's memory of driving back from Edwardian cricket parties and of the brakes packed with tired boys and girls singing as the horses trotted through the twilit Norfolk lanes. Those who have lived in country houses will have similar memories; certainly I have them myself.

Another twist, and one is looking at a way of life infinitely remote, at customs and ceremonies which seem as unlike our own experi-

(left) *View from the south portico at Stowe House, Buckinghamshire* (detail). Jacques Rigaud, c.1734.

ences as the tribal rituals in the South Sea islands. Elizabethan servants smother the food, dishes, napkins and tablecloths of their employers with ceremonial kisses; Jacobean ladies pelt each other with eggshells filled with rosewater; in the eighteenth century the Duke of Chandos sits on a marble water-closet beneath a gilded ceiling; in the nineteenth century the Duchess of Rutland's steward, riding a black horse hung with black, carries his dead mistress's coronet on a scarlet cushion; Edwardian footmen soap their hair, and then powder it with powder puffs.

Yet another twist and another change. Everything comes alive. The houses are filled with real people, often far from nice, who behave exactly like ourselves, or like people we know. House guests are bored, and bitchy about their host and hostess. Young Elizabethan bloods in Yorkshire behave just as badly as young bloods at a hunt ball today. That tough old matriarch, Bess of Hardwick, sits in her bedroom surrounded by as much clutter as a retired governess who has taken all her bits and pieces with her into a bedsitting room in North London; and, just like a retired governess eking out her gas fire, she has screens and hangings everywhere, in an endeavour to keep out the unbearable cold of Hardwick in the winter. A hundred years later Lady Gardiner complains that her stepdaughter stays out dancing all night, that her boyfriend is a bad lot, and, worst of all, that she brings his laundry back to be washed by Lady Gardiner's servants.

It is all true. Country houses and country-house life evoke a nostalgia and romanticism today – understandably so, perhaps, but to an extent of which it is easy for anyone who studies country houses to have a surfeit. For although, in some moods and under some circumstances, they are magical places, country-house life was far from pure gold all the way through.

There is a mythology of the English country house which runs something as follows. The English upper-classes, unlike their continental counterparts, have always been firmly rooted in their estates. They know the land, and enjoy its ways and its sports. They look after their tenantry and their servants, and have an easy and natural relationship with working-class people. At the same time they have a sense of duty, which leads them to devote much of their lives to public service, with no thought of personal gain. Their lives are a happy mean between country sports and pastimes, public service, and the cultivation of the mind. Their houses are filled with beautiful pictures and fine furniture. Their libraries are well stocked with books bound in vellum or tooled leather; temples and classical monuments dot their parks. They share their life with their friends, in a free hospitality which results in one of the most enviable ways of life ever devised.

Such a picture corresponds with an ideal, and the elements out of which it is made can be matched through the centuries in individual country houses or the lives of individual owners. But anyone who has studied country houses will know how often the picture is a different one. There were, and are, many dull or ugly country houses. The ideal of the great landowner who serves the public for nothing out of a sense of duty is a nineteenth-century one; most

earlier country-house owners took anything they could get out of the
public purse. The servants and dependants of country-house owners
have a way, when one can find their own comments, of turning out
much less appreciative and admiring of their employers than their
employers might like to think; and much of the prosperity and
beauty of country houses in the eighteenth and nineteenth centuries
rested on the basis of massive enclosures of agricultural land, which
reduced many agricultural workers to a life of misery and near
starvation.

Henry James's dry remark on finding the 'happy occupants' of
Wroxton Abbey away from home – 'Happy occupants, in England,
are almost always absent' – has a strong basis of truth in it. Through
the centuries country-house owners with the means to do so have
readily left their country houses, often for years at a time. They have
gone off to live in Bath or Brighton, or to travel and live on the
continent, or sail round the world; they have spent most of the year
in London, filling their houses there with fine pictures and contents
which have often ended up, in this century, in the country houses.
Some have gone away because careers in politics, government or the
armed forces took them away, others simply because they were
bored, and had the means to leave.

They were also, very often, boring. They had enough money to
do nothing, and many of them did nothing. Doing nothing is not a
recipe which produces interesting people. Staying in country houses
could be a highly enjoyable or even idyllic experience, but it could
also be, as numerous letters or descriptions testify, a dull or
disillusioning one. Accounts of this nature feature prominently in
this anthology, perhaps because accounts which have a touch of acid
in them are more entertaining to read. They should not always be
taken too seriously, however. Guests who have been invited to stay

A teaparty at Elveden Hall, Suffolk, c.1910.

with very rich or powerful people have a habit of communicating their good fortune to friends who have not been invited, but at the same time keeping their end up by not being too impressed. Raymond Asquith's comment from Chatsworth is a perfect example of this genre: 'There is only *one* bathroom in the house, which is kept for the King'.

What all this amounts to is that country-house life is and has been full of variety. It is the variety which makes it interesting. There is variety as between individual country houses and variety as between country houses of different periods: a gradual change between ideals of state and formality, which came to their peak in the seventeenth century, and ideals of informality and ease, which gradually replaced them in the course of the eighteenth and nineteenth centuries. There is the variety of different reactions, conditioned by period or background, which make the same houses fill some visitors with enthusiasm and others with indignation or disdain.

This anthology aims to give a sample of this variety. It is an invitation to enter the houses, and savour their life. Sit at the kitchen table at Knole along with Diggory Dyer, Marfidy Snipt and John Morockoe the Blackamoor. Enjoy a lively weekend with Evelyn Waugh and the Sitwells at Renishaw, where 'the household was very full of plots'. Meet the Miss Philippses at Picton Castle, 'all honest good kind of girls in their way', and Philip Morrell at Garsington 'with a glassy geniality gleaming in his eyes'. Read Elizabeth George's account of Queen Victoria at Stowe, and wonder whether, under the veil of euphemism, she is really saying that the Queen was provided with a gold chamber pot.

It is a mixed story, full of odd bits and pieces. Some are entertaining, some regrettable, some sad, some silly; but much of the story deserves the description applied to Queen Elizabeth's entertainment at Elvetham in 1591: 'The melody was sweet and the show stately'.

Blickling Hall, Norfolk, as depicted on a jug of *c*.1800.

(right) *Wisbech Castle, Cambridge* (detail). Unidentified artist, *c*.1658.

1
Arrivals
&
Impressions

*L*arge numbers of people have always been coming and going at country houses, at every kind of level. They can be heirs coming to claim their inheritance, brides coming to be married, servants coming to work, guests coming to stay or to be entertained, tenants coming to pay their rent, tradesmen coming to deliver goods or do a job, or just curious people, coming to have a look. Until lodge gates, parks and drives appeared in the eighteenth century anyone could get close to country houses, however grand, and any well-spoken person could probably get past the porter at the entrance, and have a look inside. In the eighteenth century the concept of privacy began to develop, but the same period saw the beginning of organized country-house visiting, complete with tickets, tours and guides, at a considerable number of the larger or more famous houses.

Many of these visitors left a record of their reactions or their impressions. Some produced long poems of praise or celebration, usually to please the owners; these were an especial feature of the seventeenth and early eighteenth centuries. Many wrote up the houses for publication, or committed full descriptions to their diaries or letters. Others made casual comments that can be just as revealing. Descriptions and memories can be soaked with nostalgia, or steeped in acid. Not surprisingly, the same house can provoke widely different reactions, depending on the nature of the visitor or the period of the visit.

Country and country-house pursuits on a painted screen of *c*. 1720.

(right) Porter's Lodge, Longford Castle, Wiltshire, engraved after Robert Thacker, *c*. 1860.

Ianuæ Longo Vadensis Icon; quæ Atriensi. ascribitur.

The Porters Lodg att Longford.

R. Thacker delin.   J. Collins fecit

ARRIVALS

BUT approaching to the house, being led by a large, long, straight fair way, I found a great magnificence in the front or front pieces of the house, and so every part answerable to other, to allure liking. I found no one thing of greater grace than your stately ascent from your hall to your great chamber; and your chamber answerable with largeness and lightsomeness, that truly a Momus could find no fault. I visited all your rooms, high and low, and only the contentation of mine eyes made me forget the infirmity of my legs.

LORD BURGHLEY TO SIR CHRISTOPHER HATTON, 1579

DEFOE

COMES

TO

CHATS-

WORTH

AS A

TRAVELLER

NOTHING can be more surprising of its Kind, than for a Stranger coming from the North, . . . and wandering or labouring to pass this difficult Desert Country, and feeling no End of it, and almost discouraged and beaten out with the Fatigue of it, (just such was our Case) on a sudden the Guide brings him to this Precipice, where he looks down from a frightful height, and a comfortless, barren, and, as he thought, endless Moor, into the most delightful Valley, with the most pleasant Garden, and most beautiful Palace in the World.

DANIEL DEFOE, *Tour through Great Britain* (1727)

. . . AND PAXTON AS HEAD GARDENER 1826

I left London by the Comet Coach for Chesterfield; and arrived at Chatsworth at half-past four o'clock in the morning of the ninth of May, 1826. As no person was to be seen at that early hour, I got over the greenhouse gate by the old covered way, explored the pleasure grounds and looked round the outside of the house. I then went down to the kitchen gardens, scaled the outside wall and saw the whole of the place, set the men to work there at six o'clock; then returned to Chatsworth and got Thomas Weldon to play me the water works and afterwards went to breakfast with poor dear Mrs Gregory and her niece, the latter fell in love with me and I with her, and thus completed my first morning's work, at Chatsworth before nine o'clock.

Handbook to Chatsworth and Hardwick (1845)

Belton House, Lincolnshire (detail). Unidentified artist, c. 1720.

HERE I arrived, and found the lodge; a fine old Elizabethan house, situated in as solemnly striking a solitude as one can well conceive. It stood up aloft, on a natural terrace overlooking a deep winding glen, and surrounded by sloping uplands, deep masses of wood, and the green heights of Weaver, in a situation of solitary beauty which extremely delighted me. Not a person was visible throughout the profoundly silent scene, scarcely a house was within view. I ascended to the front of the lodge, and stood in admiration of its aspect. Its tall square bulk of dark grey stone, with its turreted front, full of large square mullioned windows; its paved court, and ample flight of steps ascending to its porched door; its old garden, with terraces and pleached hedges on the south slope below it, and deep again below that, dark ponds visible amongst the wild growth of trees. The house stood, without a smoke, without a sign of life, or movement about it, in the broad sunshine of noon. I advanced and rung the bell in the porch, but no one answered it. It was, for all the world, like a hall of old romance laid under an enchanted spell. I rung again, but all was silent. I descended the flight of steps, and paced the grey pavement of the court, and was about to withdraw, when an old woman opened a casement in the storey and said, in a slow dreamy voice, 'I am coming down.'

WILLIAM HOWETT, *Visits to Remarkable Places* (1840)

15

Looking across the lake to Wilton House, Wiltshire. Detail from the painting by Richard Wilson, c. 1758.

A

NEW

DUKE

OF

PORTLAND

COMES

TO

WELBECK

ABBEY

1879

WE travelled in a saloon carriage, arriving at Worksop on a dark, windy winter evening. Outside the station there was a little crowd of people waiting to see the young Duke arrive. Their white faces and dark clothes caught the light of the dim oil lamps as they pressed round the door of the old-fashioned carriage, while my little brother Charlie was lifted carefully into a second carriage. Then a long dreary drive to Welbeck, till at last we arrived before the house. The road in front was a grass-grown morass covered with builders' rubbish, and to allow the carriage to reach the front door they had had to put down temporary planks. The hall inside was without a floor and here also planks had been laid to allow us to enter.

Why the house had been allowed to get into this state I do not know, unless it was that the old Duke was so absorbed with his vast work of digging out and building underground rooms and tunnels that he was oblivious of everything else. He pursued this hobby at the cost of every human feeling, and without any idea of beauty, a lonely, self-isolated man. It was always thought that his love of tunnels was due to a dislike of being seen. Even round the garden of Harcourt House, where he lived in London, he erected high frosted-glass screens, so that he could not be overlooked; and when he travelled he never left his own carriage, but had it placed on a railway truck at the end of the train, keeping the green silk blinds closely drawn.

Naturally rumours spread that he was a leper or suffered from some other terrible disease, but I have talked to his old servants and they tell me that he had a delicate and lovely skin, and was an extremely handsome man, tall and thin, with a proud, aristocratic air. My mother had a bust of him made from a cast after his death, and from this he certainly appears to have been a remarkably handsome man, of a thin, clear-cut type, not very unlike the Duke of Wellington, but with a harder and more selfish face.

We were met at the front door by some of the heads of departments – McCallum, the Steward, a tall Scotsman; Tinker, the Clerk of Works, and others – and shown up to the few rooms that were fit to live in. The late Duke had only inhabited four or five rooms opening into each other in the West Wing of the house. Here he lived, slept and ate; indeed, it was said that he began his nights in one room, and if unable to sleep had a bath and went into another, keeping up fires in each room. To these rooms, which were scantily and almost poorly furnished, the little family party, all dressed in black, was solemnly ushered up, and my brother Charlie was put to bed.

Next day began the journey of discovery of the house. The suite of rooms that we were living in had double sets of brass letter-boxes in the doors: one to push the letters in, and the other to push the letters out. Two of these rooms were quite charming: a large west room and a little room known as the north closet adjoining, which had

been used by the second Duchess of Portland (Matthew Prior's noble, lovely little Peggy) who brought Welbeck into the family, and was a great collector of antiques and a highly cultivated woman. It was here that she and Mrs. Delany sat, embroidered and talked. I remember the smell of these rooms now.

All the rest of the rooms in the house were absolutely bare and empty, except that almost every room had a water-closet in the corner, with water laid on and in good working order, but not enclosed or sheltered in any way. All the rooms were painted pink, and the large drawing-rooms decorated with gold; but no furniture or pictures were to be seen. At last, in a large hall, decorated rather

View from under the North Portico, Stowe House, Buckinghamshire. J.C. Nattes, 1805.

beautifully in the manner of Strawberry Hill, was found a vast gathering of cabinets all more or less in a state of disrepair.

Then on by an underground passage and up through a trap-door into the building that had originally been the Duke of Newcastle's riding school and had been lined by the late Duke with mirrors and crystal chandeliers hanging from every point of the raftered roof, which was painted to represent the bright rosy hues of sunset; but the sudden mood of gaiety that had made him decorate it as a ballroom must have soon faded, leaving the mock sunset to shine on a lonely figure reflected a hundred times in the mirrors. For stacked here were all the pictures belonging to the house – pictures that had come down from generation to generation, but taken out of their frames and set up two or three deep against gaunt 'wooden horses'. The frames were afterwards found hidden away in a storehouse.

In a similar building opposite this, which had been the stables of the Duke of Newcastle's famous horses, was the kitchen where the late Duke's perpetual chicken had been kept roasting on a spit, one chicken following another so that whenever he should call for it one should be ready roasted and fit for eating. From this kitchen the food was lowered by a lift into a heated truck that ran on rails pushed by a man through a long underground passage to the house – a method of transit which I believe still continues. Another passage branching off from this one took us to three underground rooms, all very large, and one that seemed quite immense. These also were painted pink with parquet floors; heated by hot air, and lit from the top by mushroom lights level with the ground, vast empty rooms, built down instead of up, and except for the top lighting you would not have been aware that they were under the level of the ground. Along the side of them was a glass corridor intended for statues, but with no statues.

Then back we came to the house through more underground passages. Starting from these passages was the walking tunnel, about a mile long and wide enough for two or three people to walk abreast, that led from the house to the stables and gardens; and a little way off and parallel to it was another rather rougher one for the use of the gardeners and workmen; for the Duke did not wish to meet anyone walking in the same tunnel as himself. Then there was the great driving tunnel, more than a mile long, which was the only direct road to Worksop. It had been dug out under the old drive and was wide enough for two carriages to pass each other. In the daytime it was lit from the top by small mushroom windows which threw a ghostly light upon it, except where it dipped down under the lake, and there it was lit by jets of gas, as the whole tunnel was at night.

The collection of buildings, hunting stables, riding school, coach-houses, dairy, laundry and offices with a number of cottages and a covered tan gallop, about a quarter of a mile long, made a small town in themselves. They were all built in the same grey stone in dull heavy architecture, and stood without trees or flowers – flowers indeed were banished from the place – expressing only grandeur and pomp. The riding school was said to be the largest in the world. The vegetable gardens were on an equally huge scale – a series of square gardens, each surrounded by high walls, and of an average size of about eight acres.

The poor deluded owner seemed to assert his power and pride in making all the buildings as large and lonely as possible, banishing grace and beauty and human love and companionship, and leaving his fellow-beings in order to hide in tunnels. He even cut down every tree within a considerable distance of the house.

He was kind to the hundreds of labourers who came from all the villages around to take part in these vast excavations, providing them with donkeys to carry them to and from their work, and with large silk umbrellas to shelter them from the rain.

LADY OTTOLINE MORRELL

AN

ODD

VISIT

TO

HAM

1944

I walked down the long drive to Ham House. The grounds are indescribably overgrown and unkempt. I passed long ranges of semi-derelict greenhouses. The garden is pitted with bomb craters around the house, from which a few windows have been blown out and the busts from the niches torn away. I walked round the house, which appeared thoroughly deserted, searching for an entrance. The garden and front doors looked as though they had not been used for decades. So I returned to the back door and pulled a bell. Several seconds later a feeble rusty tinkling echoed from distant subterranean regions. While waiting I recalled the grand ball given for Nefertiti Bethell which I attended in this house some ten years or more ago. The door was roughly jerked open, the bottom grating against the stone floor. The noise was accompanied by heavy breathing from within. An elderly man of sixty stood before me. He had red hair and a red face, carrot and port wine. He wore a tail coat and a starched shirt front which had come adrift from the waistcoat. 'The old alcoholic family butler,' I said to myself. He was not affable at first. Without asking my name, or business, he said, 'Follow me.' Slowly he led me down a dark passage. His legs must be webbed for he moved in painful jerks. At last he stopped outside a door, and knocked nervously. An ancient voice cried, 'Come in!' The seedy butler then said to me, 'Daddy is expecting you,' and left me. I realized that he was the bachelor son of Sir Lyonel Tollemache, aged eighty-nine. As I entered the ancient voice said, 'You can leave us alone, boy!' For a moment I did not understand that Sir Lyonel was addressing his already departed son.

Sir Lyonel was sitting in an upright chair. He was dressed, unlike his son, immaculately in a grey suit, beautifully pressed, and wore a stock tie with large pearl pin. I think he had spats over black polished shoes. A very decorative figure, and very courteous. He asked me several questions about the National Trust's scheme for preserving country houses, adding that he had not made up his mind what he ought to do. After several minutes, he rang the bell and handed me over to the son who answered it.

The son showed me hurriedly, I mean as hurriedly as he could walk, round the house, which is melancholy in the extreme.

JAMES LEES-MILNE, *Ancestral Voices*

IMPRESSIONS

Newburgh Priory, North Yorkshire. Unidentified artist, c. 1695.

THOU art not, Penshurst, built to envious show,
Of touch, or marble; nor canst boast a row
Of polish'd pillars, or a roof of gold:
Thou hast no lantern, whereof tales are told;
Or stair, or courts; but stand'st an ancient pile,
And these grudg'd at, art reverenc'd the while.
Thou joy'st in better marks, of soil, of air,
Of wood, of water: therein thou art fair.
Thou hast thy walks for health, as well as sport:
Thy Mount, to which the Dryads do resort,
Where Pan, and Bacchus their high feasts have made,
Beneath the broad beech, and the chest-nut shade;
That taller tree, which of a nut was set,
At his great birth, where all the Muses met.
There, in the writhed bark, are cut the names
Of many a Sylvan, taken with his flames.
And thence, the ruddy Satyrs oft provoke
The lighter Fauns, to reach thy Ladies oak.
Thy copse, too, nam'd of Gamage, thou hast there,
That never failes to serve thee season'd deer,
When thou would'st feast, or exercise thy friends.
The lower land, that to the river bends,
Thy sheep, thy bullocks, kine, and calves do feed:
The middle grounds thy mares, and horses breed.
Each bank doth yield thee coneyes; and the tops
Fertile of wood, Ashore, and Sydney's copse,
To crown thy open table, doth provide
The purpled pheasant, with the speckled side:
The painted partridge lies in every field,
And, for thy mess, is willing to be kill'd.
And if the high swollen Medway fail thy dish,
Thou hast thy ponds, that pay thee tribute fish,
Fat, aged carps, that run into thy net.
And pikes, now weary their own kind to eat,
As loth, the second draught, or cast to stay,
Officiously, at first, themselves betray.
Bright eels, that emulate them, and leap on land,
Before the fisher, or into his hand.
Then hath thy orchard fruit, thy garden flowers,
Fresh as the air, and new as are the hours.
The early cherry, with the later plum,
Fig, grape, and quince, each in his time doth come:
The blushing apricot, and woolly peach
Hang on thy walls, that every child may reach.
And though thy walls be of the country stone,
They're rear'd with no man's ruin, no man's groan,
There's none, that dwell about them, wish them down;
But all come in, the farmer, and the clown:
And no one empty-handed, to salute
Thy lord, and lady, though they have no suit.
Some bring a capon, some a rural cake,

Some nuts, some apples; some that think they make
The better cheeses, bring them; or else send
By their ripe daughters, whom they would commend
This way to husbands; and whose baskets bear
An emblem of themselves, in plum, or pear.
But what can this (more than expresse their love)
Add to thy free provisions, far above
The need of such? whose liberal board doth flow,
With all, that hospitality doth know!
Where comes no guest, but is allow'd to eat,
Without his fear, and of the lord's own meat:
Where the same beer, and bread, and self-same wine,
That is his Lordship's, shall be also mine.
And I not fain to sit (as some, this day,
At great men's tables) and yet dine away.
Here no man tells my cups: nor, standing by,
A waiter, doth my gluttony envy:
But gives me what I call, and lets me eat,
He knows, below, he shall find plenty of meat,
Thy tables hoard not up for the next day,
Nor, when I take my lodging, need I pray
For fire, or lights, or liver: all is there;
As if thou, then, wert mine, or I reign'd here:
There's nothing I can wish, for which I stay.
That found King James, when hunting late, this way,
With his brave son, the Prince, they saw thy fires
Shine bright on every hearth as the desires
Of thy Penates had been set on flame,
To entertain them; or the country came,
With all their zeal, to warm their welcome here.
What (gear, I will not say, but) sudden cheer
Did'st thou, then, make them! and what praise was heap'd
On thy good lady, then! who, therein, reap'd
The just reward of her high housewifery;
To have her linen, plate, and all things nigh,
When she was far: and not a room, but dressed
As if it had expected such a guest!
These, Penshurst, are thy praise, and yet not all.
Thy lady's noble, fruitful, chaste withal.
His children thy great lord may call his own:
A fortune, in this age, but rarely known.
They are, and have been taught religion: Thence
Their gentler spirits have suck'd innocence.
Each morn, and even, they are taught to pray,
With the whole household, and may, every day,
Read, in their virtuous parent's noble parts,
The mysteries of manners, armies, and arts.
Now, Penshurst, they that will proportion thee
With other edifices, when they see
Those proud, ambitious heaps, and nothing else,
May say, their lords have built, but thy lord dwells.

BEN JONSON, *To Penshurst*

HIGHER yet in the very East frontier of this county, upon a rough and a craggy soil standeth Hardwick, which gave name to a family which possessed the same: out of which descended Lady Elizabeth Countess of Shrewsbury, who began to build there two goodly houses joining in a manner one to the other, which by reason of their lofty situation show themselves a far off to be seen, and yield a very goodly prospect.

WILLIAM CAMDEN, *Britannia, translated Holland* (1610)

Never was I less charmed in my life. The house is not Gothic, but of that betweenity, that intervened when Gothic declined and Palladian was creeping in – rather, this is totally naked of either ... The gallery is sixty yards long, covered with bad tapestry and wretched pictures.

HORACE WALPOLE, 1760

Some of the Apartments are large, but ill fitted up, & the general Disposition of the Rooms is awkward ... I took notice of a good deal of old Stucco in the State Room representing Hastings, & the figures coloured, but it is very ugly.

PHILIP YORKE, LORD HARDWICKE, 1763

Like a great old castle of romance ... Such lofty magnificence! And built with stone, upon a hill! One of the proudest piles I ever beheld.

JOHN BYNG, LORD TORRINGTON, 1789

... at about 10 we set off [from Chatsworth] for Hardwick Hall ... arrived at about 1, and went over the house which is very curious and old but yet so *liveable* that it looks as if it was not so old as it is.

Extract from Princess Victoria's Journal, Monday, 22 October, 1832

We went to Hardwick – a vilely ugly house but full of good needlework.

EVELYN WAUGH, *Diary,* 1930

We turn round and there Hardwick stands before us at another angle, and we see the lead statues and yew alleys of its haunted garden. To what can we compare it? To Chambord, but only for its fantastic roof, where the ladies sat to watch François Premier hunting in the forest. Not for its interior beauties, for it has none, except the twisting stairway. Yet Chambord is the most beautiful of the French châteaux. The only great house of the Renaissance to which Hardwick could be compared is Caprarola; but its faded frescoes of the Farnese family are as nothing to this hunting frieze; the moss-grown giants, the tritons and Atlantes, are not more magical than the needlework, more romantic than the hand of Mary Stuart; even the faun caryatids, mysteriously smiling, under the full baskets of ripe figs and grapes upon their heads, some of them whispering to their neighbour statue, are not more beautiful than Summer resting on the corn stooks, to watch the golden harvest. From Caprarola you can see Soracte and the Volscian mountains. The dome of St. Peter's floats in the distance over Rome. But we would sooner the view of the collieries outside the park. What wonders we have come from! All hidden, all enclosed behind the leaded windows, under the towers of Hardwick, looking out for all weathers on the stag-antlered trees.

SACHEVERELL SITWELL, *British Architects and Craftsmen* (1945)

It is of a consistency and hardness which must have suited the old woman entirely. And as the house stands on the flattened top of the hill, there is nothing of surrounding nature either that could compete with its uncompromising unnatural, graceless, and indomitable self-assertiveness. It is an admirable piece of design and architectural expression: no fussing, no fumbling, nor indeed any flights of fancy.

NIKOLAUS PEVSNER, *The Buildings of England* (1953)

Elizabeth, Countess of Shrewsbury ('Bess of Hardwick'). Detail from the portrait at Hardwick.

POPE

MAKES

FUN

OF

BLENHEIM

SEE, sir, here's the grand approach,
This way is for his Grace's coach;
There lies the bridge, and here's the clock,
Observe the lion and the cock,
The spacious court, the colonnade,
And mark how wide the hall is made!
The chimneys are so well design'd,
They never smoke in any wind.
This gallery's contriv'd for walking,
The windows to retire and talk in;
The council chamber for debate,
And all the rest are rooms of state.
Thanks, sir, cried I, 'tis very fine,
But where d'ye sleep, or where d'ye dine?
I find by all you have been telling
That 'tis a house, but not a dwelling.

ALEXANDER POPE (attributed), *Upon the Duke of*
Marlborough's House at Woodstock

WALPOLE

IS

AMAZED

BY

CASTLE

HOWARD

1772

NOBODY had told me that I should at one view see a palace, a town, a fortified city, temples on high places, woods worthy of being each a metropolis of the Druids, the noblest lawn in the world fenced by half the horizon, and a mausoleum that would tempt one to be buried alive; in short I have seen gigantic places before but never a sublime one.

HORACE WALPOLE TO GEORGE
SELWYN, AUGUST 12, 1772

...BUT PRINCE PÜCKLER-MUSKAU IS LESS
IMPRESSED 1827
On my journey I visited Castle Howard, the seat of Lord Carlisle. It is one of the English 'show places', but does not please me in the least. It was built by Vanbrugh, an architect of the time of Louis the Fourteenth, who built Blenheim in the same bad French taste. That, however, imposes by its mass, but Castle Howard neither imposes nor

(right) Badminton House, Gloucestershire. Detail from the painting by Antonio Canaletto, 1748.

pleases. The whole park, too, has something to the last degree melancholy, stiff, and desolate. On a hill is a large temple, the burial-place of the family. The coffins are placed around in cells, most of which are still empty; so that the whole looks like a bee-hive, only indeed more silent and tranquil.

The park, planted in large stiff masses, is re-markably rich in arch-ways: I passed through about seven before I reached the house. Over a muddy pond, not far from the Castle, is a stone bridge of five or six arches, and over this bridge – no passage. It is only an 'object'; and that it may answer this description thoroughly, there is not a tree or a bush near it or before it. It seems that the whole grounds are just as they were laid out a hundred and twenty years ago. Obelisks and pyramids are as thick as hops, and every view ends with one, as a staring termination. One pyramid is, however, of use, for it is an inn.

PÜCKLER-MUSKAU, *Tour* (1830)

LOWTHER! in thy majestic Pile are seen
Cathedral pomp and grace, in apt accord
With the baronial castle's sterner mien;
Union significant of God adored,
And charters won and guarded by the sword
Of ancient honour; whence that goodly state
Of polity which wise men venerate,
And will maintain, if God his help afford.
Hourly the democratic torrent swells;
For airy promises and hopes suborned
The strength of backward-looking thoughts is
    scorned.
Fall if ye must, ye Towers and Pinnacles,
With what ye symbolise; authentic Story
Will say, Ye disappeared with England's Glory!

WILLIAM WORDSWORTH, *Itinerary Poems* (1833)

MEMORIES

OF

WESTACRE

HIGH

HOUSE

C. 1890

THE house itself somehow seemed full of significance, tinged with melancholy, and steeped in romance; the owls always hooted there in the evenings, there were always white tobacco-plants planted under the windows. It was a very big house, grey, and spreading itself about, with a gallery stretching from one end of it to the other – a place of ample fire-places and log fires, comfort and warmth, the browns and reds of leather chairs, and dark pictures in gilt frames, with a piano at one end and untidy pile of music on the ottoman beside it. The stables were full of horses, the kennels full of greyhounds; from the windows one used to watch a party going off cubbing or hunting, and the dog-boys leading a string of greyhounds across the rather bare and ragged park. Hunting, the famous partridge-shooting, and cricket marked the seasons very distinctly.

CONSTANCE SITWELL, *Bright Morning*

AND what shall I say of the colour of Wroxton Abbey, which we visited last in order and which in the thickening twilight, as we approached its great ivy-muffled face, laid on the mind the burden of its felicity? Wroxton Abbey, as it stands, is a house of about the same period as Compton Wynyates – the latter years, I suppose, of the sixteenth century. But it is quite another affair. The place is inhabited, 'kept up', full of the most interesting and most splendid detail. Its happy occupants, however, were fortunately not in the act of staying there (happy occupants, in England, are almost always absent), and the house was exhibited with a civility worthy of its merit. Everything that in the material line can render life noble and charming has been gathered into it with a profusion which makes the whole place a monument to past opportunity. As I wandered from one rich room to another and looked at these things, that intimate appeal to the romantic sense which I just mentioned was mercilessly emphasised. But who can tell the story of the romantic sense when that adventurer really rises to the occasion – takes its ease in an old English country-house while the twilight darkens the corners of expressive rooms and the victim of the scene, pausing at the window, turns his glance from the observing portrait of a handsome ancestral face and sees the great soft billows of the lawn melt away into the park?

HENRY JAMES, *English Hours*

THOSE serene country houses of pre-war years! Looking back at them, they seem to swim in a haze of sunshine and ease, their parks with the light striking across the slopes of open grass as one drove up to the door in the evenings; trout streams, and king-cups, and shallow fords with the cows standing knee-deep in the water; someone fishing in the distance, the sinking sun flushing trees and sward with rich gold green; gardens and familiar gardeners who looked just the same year after year; ancient mulberry trees with their branches propped up from below; bee-hives in a row in the orchard; the mossy broken-down seats in shrubberies. How much indeed of the summer holidays passed going into the garden, pinching and eating fruit; the plums and greengages were visited every day, and the ground in front of them became worn into a path; the leisurely, laughing tennis; the slippery polished staircases and halls, which smelt of bees-wax and azaleas; the big tables with hats and sticks and hunting crops and fishing-rods laid on them and, when one looked out of the window after coming up to bed, there was a twilight lawn and the incense of the evening came up, breathed from garden and grass-land and streams far and near.

CONSTANCE SITWELL, *Bright Morning*

THE
DUCHESS
OF
DEVONSHIRE
ON
CHATSWORTH
1984

THE charm, attraction, character, call it what you will, of the house is that it has grown over the years in a haphazard sort of way. Nothing fits exactly, none of the rooms except the Chapel is a set-piece, like those in many houses which were built and furnished by one man in the fashion of one time. It is a conglomeration of styles and periods, of furniture and decoration. You find a hideous thing next to a beautiful thing, and since taste is intensely personal you would probably disagree with me as to which is which. It is a decorator's nightmare, unless that decorator has exceptionally catholic taste. There is no theme, no connecting style. Each room is a jumble of old and new, English and foreign, thrown together by generations of acquisitive inhabitants and standing up to change by the variety of its proportions and the strength of its cheerful atmosphere.

Likewise the outside. There is something surprising to see wherever you look; nothing can be taken for granted. Some of the house is like a mongrel dog, bits too long and bits too short, a beautiful head with an out of scale tail, and in the garden there are buildings and ornaments of so many dates and tastes you begin to wonder who was in charge here and when.

DEBORAH, DUCHESS OF DEVONSHIRE, *The House*

(right) The Harden family at Brathay Hall, Westmorland. John Harden, 1810.

2
The
Family

Mr and Mrs Tasburgh, of Burghwallis Hall in Yorkshire, lived seven years in the same house without meeting or speaking to each other. The only contact between them was when Mr Tasburgh was walking on the lawn outside the house; his wife would lean out of her bedroom window to spit on him. She had been an heiress, and they were at odds about her property.

Owning land dominated the lives of country-house families. It made them the feudal, or semi-feudal, overlords of hundreds or even thousands of people. Land was the basis of their power and wealth, a frequent reason for their marriages, a source of feuds between families and within families. Buying and selling land, improving it, planting it, farming it or hunting over it, occupied much of their time.

But their wealth and their position as a ruling class constantly pulled them away from their land – to attend court, or parliament, or the London season, to fill government offices, to travel, or just to have a good time. All kinds of options were open to them, and all kinds of different families resulted. There were hunting and shooting families, political families, intellectual families, domestic families and dissipated families. There were families who never went to London, families who seldom left it, and families who vanished for years to Europe. There were wives who went one way, and husbands another. In most counties there were one or two notably 'clever' families, such as the Trevelyans in Northumberland, who were looked at a little askance by their sporting neighbours. All kinds met constantly together, in country or London society, knew each other, criticized each other, and gossiped about each other.

In the background lurked an ideal of perfect balance between town and country, sport and culture, responsibility and fun. A few families or individuals came close to reaching it. Lord Egremont was one, except perhaps for his string of illegitimate children – owner of Petworth, paternal landlord of many thousand acres, patron of Turner and other artists, tireless sportsman, genial host, individual to the point of eccentricity. But eccentricity has always been tolerated in country houses, and the space, time, money and deference built into their way of life has even encouraged it. If the fifth Duke of Portland chose to go underground like a millionaire mole, no-one was going to stop him.

Elizabeth Spencer was a great heiress, the daughter of an extremely rich London merchant, and was in a strong bargaining position.

ELIZABETH SPENCER MAKES THINGS CLEAR TO HER FIANCÉ LORD COMPTON 1594

MY sweet life, Now I have declared to you my mind for the settling of your estate, I suppose that it were best for me to bethink and consider within myself what allowance were meetest for me ... I pray and beseech you to grant to me, your most kind and loving wife, the sum of £2600. quarterly to be paid. Also I would, besides that allowance, have £600. quarterly to be paid, for the performance of charitable works; and those things I would not, neither will be accountable for. Also, I will have three horses for my own saddle, that none shall dare to lend or borrow: none lend but I, none borrow but you.

Also, I would have two gentlewomen, lest one should be sick, or have some other let. Also, believe it, it is an undecent thing for a gentlewoman to stand mumping alone, when God hath blessed their lord and lady with a great estate. Also, when I ride a hunting, or a hawking, or travel from one house to another, I will have them attending; so, for either of those said women, I must and will have for either of them a horse. Also, I will have six or eight gentlemen; and I will have my two coaches, one lined with velvet to myself, with four very fair horses; and a coach for my women, lined with cloth and laced with gold, or otherwise with scarlet and laced with silver, with four good horses.

Also, I will have two coachmen; one for my own coach, the other for my women. Also, at any time when I travel, I will be allowed not only caroches and spare horses, for me and my women, and I will have such carriages as be fitting for all, orderly, not pestering my things with my women's, nor theirs with either chambermaids, nor theirs with washmaids. Also, for laundresses, when I travel, I will have them sent away before with the carriages, to see all safe. And the chambermaids I will have go before, that the chamber may be ready, sweet and clean. Also, that it is undecent for me to crowd up myself with my gentleman-usher in my coach, I will have him to have a convenient horse to attend me, either in city or country. And I must have two footmen. And my desire is, that you defray all the charges for me. And for myself besides my yearly allowance, I would have twenty gowns of apparel; six of them excellent good ones, eight of them for the country, and six other of them very excellent good ones. Also, I would have to put in my purse £2000 and £200, and so, you to pay my debts. Also I would have £6000 to buy me jewels; and £4000 to buy me a pearl chain.

Now, seeing I have been, and am so reasonable unto you, I pray you do find my children apparel, and their schooling, and all my servants, men and women, their wages. Also, I will have all my

(left) Sir Thomas Cave of Stanford Hall, Leicestershire, and family, c. 1770. Silhouette by Toroend.
Elizabeth Vernon, Countess of Southampton. Unidentified artist, c. 1600.

'Fledges' are probably pillows or quilts filled with feathers or down. 'Darnix' is a fabric originally made in Tournai, probably of wool and linen. 'Fustian' is a cloth or cloth blanket with a linen warp and cotton weft.

BESS OF HARDWICK'S BEDROOM 1601

IN my Lady's Bed Chamber: two pieces of tapestry hangings with people and forest work fifteen feet and a half deep, a bedstead, the posts being covered with scarlet laid on with silver lace, bed head, tester and single valance of scarlet, the valance embroidered with gold studs and tassels, striped down and laid about with gold and silver lace and with gold fringe about, three Curtains of scarlet striped down with silver lace and with silver and red silk buttons and loops, five Curtains of purple baize, a mattress, a featherbed, a bolster, a pillow, two little pillows, two quilts whereof one linen, the other candlewick, three pairs of fustians, Six spanish blankets, eight fledges about the bed, two Curtains of red Cloth for the windows, three Coverlets to hang before a window, a Coverlet to hang before a door, a Counterpoint of tapestry before another door, a cupboard inlaid and Carved, a little folding table, a turkey Carpet to it, a chair of russet satin striped with silver and with silver and russet silk fringe, two foot-stools of wood, two foot Carpets of turkey work, a covering for the russet satin Chair of scarlet embroidered with flowers of petit point, a stool and a footstool of scarlet suitable to the same, a high joined stool, two other Joined stools, an inlaid stool.

A long cushion of cloth of gold on both sides, a long cushion of needlework of Crewel with pansies and lined with green says, a little needlework cushion with my Lady's Arms in it lined with red velvet, my Lady's books viz: Calvin upon Job, covered with russet velvet, the resolution, Solomon's proverbs, a book of meditations, two other books covered with black velvet, a looking glass, an hour glass, two brushes, a pair of pulleys lined with black taffeta, a great Iron Chest painted, three great trunks, two little trunks, three Desks covered with leather whereof one a great one, a little desk to write on gilded, a little Coffer gilt, a little Coffer covered with leather, a little Coffer covered in black velvet, three flat Coffers covered

houses furnished, and my lodging chambers to be suited with all such furniture as is fit; as beds, stools, chairs, suitable cushions, carpets, silver warming-pans, cupboards of plate, fair hangings, and such like. So for my drawing-chamber in all houses, I will have them delicately furnished, both with hangings, couch, canopy, glass, carpet, chairs, cushions, and all things thereunto belonging. Also, my desire is, that you would pay your debts, build up Ashby house and purchase lands, and lend no money, as you love God, to my lord chamberlain, who would have all, perhaps your life from you . . .

So, now that I have declared to you what I would have, and what it is that I would not have, I pray you, when you be an earl, to allow me £2000 more than I now desire, and double attendance.

HARLEIAN MSS.

Perseverance, attendant to Penelope. Detail from the 'Heroines and Virtues' embroideries at Hardwick Hall.

Col. Pl. I (top) Barbara, Lady Sidney, with six children. Marcus Gheeraerts the Younger, 1596.

Col. Pl. II Lord and Lady Beauchamp and family in the staircase hall at Madresfield Court, Worcestershire. W.B. Ranken, 1924.

with leather, a box painted and gilded with my Lord's and my Lady's Arms on it, a Yellow Cotton to cover it, an other box covered with green velvet, two trussing Coffers bound with Iron, five wood boxes, a wicker screen, a pair of Copper Andirons, a pair of Iron Andirons, a fire shovel, a pair of tongs, a pair of bellows, My Lady Arbell's bedstead, a Canopy of darnix blue and white with gilt knobs and blue and white fringe, a Cloth of Checker work of Crewel about the bed, a mattress, a feather bed, a bolster, a quilt, four spanish blankets, a pair of fustians. In a pallet there: a mattress, a featherbed, two bolsters, two blankets, a Coverlet, wainscot under the windows.

HARDWICK INVENTORY

Lady Gardiner describes the behaviour of her stepdaughter Ursula Stewkeley at Preshaw, Hampshire.

TROUBLE WITH THE YOUNGER GENERATION 1674

I wish he [her husband] had stayed at home, but your sex will follow their inclinations which is not for women's convenience. I should be more contented if his daughter Ursula were not here, who after 8 month's pleasure came home unsatisfied, declaring Preshaw was never so irksome to her, and now hath been at all the Salisbury races, dancing like wild with Mr Clark whom Jack can give you a character of, and came home of a Saturday night just before our Winton [Winchester] races, at near 12 o'clock when my family was abed, with Mr Charles Turner (a man I know not, Judge Turner's son, who was tried for his life last November for killing a man, one of the number that styles themselves Tyburn Club), and Mr Clark's brother, who sat up 2 nights till near 3 o'clock, and said she had never been in bed since she went away till 4 in the morning, and danced some nights till 7 in the morning. Then she borrowed a coach and went to our races, and would have got dancers if she could, then brought home this crew with her again, and sat up the same time. All this has sufficiently vexed me.

Her father was 6 days of this time from home, and she lay out 3 nights of it, and Friday she was brought home and brought with her Mr Turner's linen to be mended and washed here and sent after him to London, where he went on Saturday, to see how his brother Mun is come of his trial for killing a man just before the last circuit. And since these were gone, I reflecting on these actions, and she declaring she could not be pleased on the 24, and taking it ill I denied in my husband's absence to have 7 ranting fellows come to Preshaw to bring music, was very angry and had ordered where they should all lie, she designed me to lie with Peg G., and I scaring her and contradicting her, we had a great quarrel.

LADY GARDINER TO HER BROTHER, SIR RALPH VERNEY, 4 MAY, 1674

Col. Pl. III (top left) The Sneyd family dancing in the hall at Keele Hall, Staffordshire, 1882.
Col. Pl. IV (left) Sir Rowland and Lady Winn in the library at Nostell Priory, Yorkshire. Unidentified artist, c.1767.
(above) Sir John Trevelyan of Wallington Hall, Northumberland, and his family. Arthur Devis, c. 1770.

A

DUKE

AND

DUCHESS

AT

HOME:

THE

BEAUFORTS

AT

BADMINTON

1680

AS for the duke and duchess, and their friends, there was no time of the day without diversion. Breakfast in her gallery that opened into the gardens; then, perhaps, a deer was to be killed, or the gardens, and parks, with the several sort of deer, to be visited; and if it required mounting, horses of the duke were brought for all the company. And so, in the afternoon, when the ladies were disposed to air, and the gentlemen with them, coaches and six came to hold them all. At half an hour after eleven the bell rang to prayers, so at six in the evening; and, through a gallery, the best company went into an aisle in the church (so near was it), and the duke could see if all the family were there. The ordinary pastime of the ladies was in a gallery on the other side, where she had divers gentlewomen commonly at work upon embroidery and fringe-making; for all the beds of state were made and finished in the house.

ROGER NORTH. *Lives of the Norths*

AN iron stove w. furniture, 1 Moon Lanthorne, 1 steel crossbow, a iron chest, 1 old squab and cushion, 1 table, 3 cane chairs, 1 old green cushion, 1 pair of old window curtains and rod, 10 pairs of leather bags, 5 dozen money bags, 1 portmanteau, a male pillion, 3 trooping saddles & bridles, housing & holsters, 3 pad saddles, 1 snaffle bridle, 1 fine saddle with red embroidered furniture, & the furniture of a saddle of blue with gold embroidery, 2 tin money shovels and a chain to measure land, 2 swords, 1 sumpter saddle, 1 bridle and 2 hampers.

INVENTORY OF LANGLEYS, ESSEX

(right) Catherine Allan at Brathay Hall. John Harden, 1805

AN

EVENING

WITH

SIR

JOHN

PHILIPPS

AND

HIS

FAMILY

AT

PICTON

CASTLE

PEMBROKESHIRE

1754

THE cloth was just gone, and the clock had struck ten
When Moll, who hates idleness, took up a pen;
No aid she implored, no muse she'd invoke,
For she never attempted to write save in joke.
The subject she chose was her friends round the fire,
For her genius, alas! would never reach higher.
The party consisted of no more than five,
And a list'ner would scarcely have thought them alive,
Such undisturbed silence there reigned, so profound,
That no mortal creature could hear the least sound.
The Knight, as superior, first appears on the stage,
He was carefully turning o'er many a page
While sleep did her Ladyship kindly engage.
The next were her daughters, nor handsome nor gay,
But all honest good kind of girls in their way.
I have only a right to precedence by birth,
I'm honest and free, and love innocent mirth,
And freely submit to my sisters in worth,
Miss Betty all meekness and mildness, and merit,
Miss Kitty, though good, has a little more spirit.
So much for their characters; now I'm to say
How they were employed; not in romping and play,
But instead of all that, and flirting and stuff,
Miss Betty was dextrously making a ruff.
And instead of crying eagerly, who'd cut old shuffle,
Miss Kitty was busily altering a ruffle.
While silently thus our time steals away
We're envied by none, and despised by the gay.
But my comfort is this, we *may* make good wives,
For men say that flirts are the plague of their lives.
Now Sir John shuts his book, and my Lady's awake,
The chambermaid's called for the candles to take.
My pen I must quit, to wish you good night,
May I give you more pleasure the next time I write.

From a Poem by Molly Philipps

A girl tries on her mother's garland. Watercolour by one of the Drummond children, of Denham, Buckinghamshire, c. 1830.

... **A**ND this day we have been all sitting together in the drawing room going on with our various little employments – Mrs Sneyd by turns making net for one of the Miss Leicester's and a pantin [puppet] for one of the Leicester children – Emma rummaging in a box for new ribbons from Lichfield to find what will suit half a dozen nets – all the ribbons so pretty that they make ones eyes water – Fanny in the library by her recluse philosophical self for some time – Then joining the vulgar herd in the drawing room – Honora on Fanny's appearance quitting her drawing table where she was copying Mr. J. Sneyd's Captain Moneygawl and joining Fanny on the sofa and reading out of one book (and that book too small for any one person) Ariosto, translating it much to their mutual satisfaction both saying the lines at a time and hoping 'Aunt Sneyd and Maria we don't disturb you' ...

Enter Mr Sneyd, to whom as if he was just landed from Naples both the Italian scholars ran with their book and 'Oh uncle! Oh Mr. Sneyd! You'll explain this' ...

Luncheon – damson pie – pork pie – mutton steaks – hot mashed potatoes – puffs – unnoticed – brawn untouched – cold roast beef on sideboard – seen to late! Observation by Mrs Sneyd – Not well bred ever you know to put the gravy on the meat when you serve anybody – No because you should leave the person at liberty to eat it or not as they please.

MARIA EDGEWORTH

SUCH is Lord Egremont. Literally like the sun. The very flies at Petworth seem to know there is room for their existence, that the windows are theirs. Dogs, horses, cows, deer and pigs, peasantry and servants, guests and family, children and parents, all share alike his bounty and opulence and luxuries. At breakfast, after the guests have all breakfasted, in walks Lord Egremont; first comes a grandchild, whom he sends away happy. Outside the window moan a dozen black spaniels, who are let in, and to them he distributes cakes and comfits, giving all equal shares. After chatting with one guest, and proposing some scheme of pleasure to others, his leather gaiters are buttoned on, and away he walks, leaving everybody to take care of themselves, with all that opulence and generosity can place at their disposal entirely within their reach. At dinner he meets everybody, and then are recounted the feats of the day. All principal dishes he helps, never minding the trouble of carving; he eats heartily and helps liberally. There is plenty, but not absurd profusion; good wines, but not extravagant waste. Everything solid, liberal, rich and English. At seventy-four he still shoots daily, comes home wet through, and is as active and looks as well as many men of fifty.

BENJAMIN ROBERT HAYDEN, *Journals*

TWO GENERATIONS AT WALLINGTON 1862

SEPT. 24. – Sir Walter is a strange-looking being, with long hair and moustache, and an odd careless dress. He also has the reputation of being a miser. He is a great teetotaller, and inveighs everywhere against wine and beer: I trembled as I ran the gauntlet of public opinion yesterday in accepting a glass of sherry. Lady Trevelyan is a great artist. She is a pleasant, bright little woman, with sparkling black eyes, who paints beautifully, is intimately acquainted with all the principal artists, imports baskets from Madeira and lace from Honiton, and sells them in Northumberland, and always sits upon the rug by preference.

Blind man's buff. Water-colour by one of the Drummon children, c. 1830.

Sept. 26. – Such a curious place this is! and such curious people! I get on better with them now, and even Sir Walter is gruffly kind and grumpily amiable. As to information, he is a perfect mine, and he knows every book and ballad that ever was written, every story of local interest that ever was told, and every flower and fossil that ever was found – besides the great-grandfathers and great-grandmothers of everybody dead or alive. His conversation is so curious that I follow him about everywhere, and take notes under his nose, which he does not seem to mind in the least, but only says something more quaint and astonishing the next minute. Lady Trevelyan is equally unusual. She is abrupt to a degree, and contradicts everything. Her little black eyes twinkling with mirth all day long, though she says she is ill and has 'the most extraordinary *feels*;' she is 'sure no one ever had such extraordinary feels as she has.' She never appears to attend to her house a bit, which is like a great desert with one or two little oases in it, where by good management you may possibly make yourself comfortable. She paints foxgloves in fresco and makes little sketches à la Ruskin in the tiniest of books.

AUGUSTUS HARE, *The Story of my Life*

.... AND 1940

Lady Trevelyan speaks succinctly, carefully and measuredly, using the north country clipped 'a', and is distinctly 'clever'. Gertrude Bell was her sister. Lady T. is handsome in a 'no nonsense about appearances' manner, and looks as though she may have been the first woman chairman of the L.C.C. I don't know if she ever was this. She is authoritarian, slightly deaf, and wears pince-nez. The two daughters are abrupt and rather terrifying. Mrs. Dower paints water-colours, competently. After dinner I am worn out, and long for bed. But no. We have general knowledge questions. Lady T. puts the questions one after the other with lightning rapidity. I am amazed and impressed by her mental agility, and indeed by that of the daughters, who with pursed lips shoot forth unhesitating answers like a spray of machine-gun bullets. All most alarming to a tired stranger. At the end of the 'game', for that is what they call this preparatory school examination, they allot marks. Every single member of the family get 100 out of 100. The son-in-law gets 80, Matheson (who is also a clever man) gets 30. I get 0.

JAMES LEES-MILNE, *Ancestral Voices*

Playing billiards in the long gallery, Capesthorne, Cheshire. James Johnson, c. 1840 (detail).
(right) A corner of the library at Wootton Hall, Staffordshire. Detail from an anonymous water-colour, c. 1850.

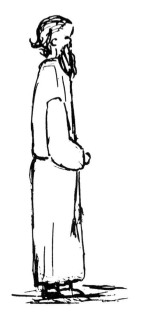

THE

BUXTONS

AT

NORTH-

REPPS

1864

THEN every evening we used to go up to bed at 10, when we reached the landing Granny used to sit down on a chair, and we all stood round and gossiped, perhaps for ten minutes or a quarter of an hour, quite a large party of us, then we all used to go away into our rooms, my Mother used to go away into her room, Pris into hers, Granny into hers, Aunt Emily into hers, Sally into hers and me into mine, and when we were all undressed and in our neat dressing gowns we used again to go and see one another once or twice before we got into bed. Even Uncle Charles used to come and see us, in his dressing-gown, looking more like a man in Noah's Ark than anything else I have ever seen. I have drawn a picture of him, and Father used to come and see us too but he didn't look so much like a man in Noah's Ark because he hasn't got a long beard like Uncle Charles.

ELLEN BUXTON, *Diary*

SIR

ROUNDELL

PALMER

MOVES

INTO

HIS

NEW

HOUSE

AT prayers where we mustered now a large party before kneeling down R. made one of his nice addresses to the whole household, explaining how he came to be in possession by God's blessing on his labour, that we were to remember that we were the first to come and live here, that we must not only try to be a help to our poor neighbours, but examples too and that as there would be always plenty *in* the house he wished never to see or hear of any one of his servants being seen or heard of at a public house – he did it kindly but very firmly.

DIARY OF LADY PALMER, BLACKMOOR HOUSE, HAMPSHIRE, 19 OCTOBER, 1866

THE COUNTESS OF CARDIGAN AT DEENE C. 1900

As she grew older her clothes became most remarkable. Some neighbours, calling on her at Deene, found her dressed in Lord Cardigan's red military riding trousers and cuirass with a leopard skin thrown over her shoulders. Her visitors looked rather surprised at this get up, and were still more astonished when she told them it was her bicycling costume! Sometimes she would come down attired as a Spanish dancer, with a coloured skirt covered with lace and a mantilla and high comb, when she would dance the cachoncha, playing the castanets with great skill and verve. Another evening she would flit round the great hall dressed like the Grey Nun who was supposed to haunt the place, when it behoved her guests to show alarm by hiding under the tables and chairs. In every-day life she wore a wig composed of golden curls with a scarlet geranium fixed behind her ear. Many years after she had given up riding she would drive to the Meet in her brougham dressed for hunting in a smart habit and high hat. Stepping lightly out of her carriage she would survey the scene, and then remark to anyone near her that her stupid groom had taken her horse to the wrong Meet. For several years before her death she kept her coffin in the inner hall and would order her butler, Knighton, to lift her into it so that she might be certain that it was comfortable.

LADY AUGUSTA FANE, *Chit-Chat*

(left) Uncle Charles Buxton in his dressing gown, and the Buxton children reciting verses to Papa. Drawings by Ellen Buxton, 1864 and 1865.
(above) The Duchess of Marlborough in her boudoir at Blenheim. George Scharf, 1864.

'LADY Astor was always immaculate in appearance, and she took a pride in being so. She treated her clothes well and was very tidy. When she changed she hung her discarded clothes on a hanger, put her hat on the hat stand and trees in her shoes. She was particularly fastidious about her underwear. It was kept in sets in silk pouches which I had to make and decorate in his lordship's racing colours, blue and pink. Every evening I would leave one pouch on her stool and she would fold her underwear into it and tie the ribbon, and so it would be sent to be laundered ... Her ladyship's underwear was hand made in France, at some school for crippled girls, from a silk and wool mixture for winter, with knickers fitting above the knee, and of triple ninon for the summer, beautifully appliquéd and sewn.

R. HARRISON *Rose: My Life In Service*

The 3rd Lord Leconfield in the garden at Petworth, c. 1950.
(right) the 9th Duke of Devonshire and seventeen grandchildren at Chatsworth, Christmas, 1931.

STATELY and strange it stood, the Nabob's house,
Indian without and coolest Greek within,
Looking from Gloucestershire to Oxfordshire;
And, by supremest landscape-gardener's art,
The lake below the eastward slope of grass
Was made to seem a mighty river-reach
Curving along to Chipping Norton's hills.
    Crackle of gravel! in the entrance-hall
Boot-jacks and mattocks, hunting mackintosh,
And whips and sticks and barometric clock
Were Colonel Dugdale's; but a sheaf of bast
And gardening-basket told us of his wife.
'Camilla Russell – Bridget King-Tenison –
And Major Attlee – Patsy Rivington –
Shall we go in? I think it's rather late.'
    Dear Mrs Dugdale, mother of us all,
In trailing and Edwardian-looking dress,
A Sargent portrait in your elegance,
Sweet confidante in every tale of woe!
She and her son and we were on the Left,
But Colonel Dugdale was Conservative.
From one end of the butler-tended board
The Colonel's eyes looked out towards the hills,
While at the other end our hostess heard
Political and undergraduate chat.
'Oh, Ethel,' loudly Colonel Dugdale's voice
Boomed sudden down the table, 'that manure –
I've had it shifted to the strawberry-beds.'
'Yes, Arthur . . . Major Attlee, as you said,
Seventeen million of the poor Chinese
Eat less than half a calory a week?'
        How proud beneath the swelling dome
            I sang Lord Ullin's daughter
        At Mrs Dugdale's grand At Home
            To Lady Horsbrugh-Porter
So Sezincote became a second home.

The love between those seeming opposites,
Colonel and Mrs Dugdale, warmed their guests.
The paddock where the Colonel's favourite mare,
His tried companion of the '14 war,
Grazed in retirement – what is in it now?
New owners wander to the Temple Pool
Where Mrs Dugdale snipped exotic shrubs
With secateurs as on and on I talked.
The onion dome which listened all the time
To water filling after-tennis baths,
To water splashing over limestone rock
Under the primulas and thin bamboo,
The cottages and lanes and woods and paths
Are all so full of voices from the past
I do not dare return.

JOHN BETJEMAN, *Summoned by Bells*

Mrs Ronald Greville on the verandah at Polesden Lacey,
Surrey, c. 1940.
(right) Arthur Williams-Wynn learning to ride a bicycle when
staying at Milton House, Northamptonshire, c. 1890.

3
Guests

*H*aving people to stay is made easy when there is abundance of space and servants. Since both were to be found in country houses, guests have featured prominently in country-house life from the Middle Ages onwards. To begin with, when roads were almost non-existent, distances great, and horse or foot the only means of transport, anyone who came to a house on business or for a meal almost automatically stayed the night. This was less the case as transport improved, but on the other hand improved transport made it easier to bring invited guests across long distances for short periods. The coming of the railways marked the great breakthrough. As a result it was in nineteenth-century country-houses that the house-party entered on its apogee, especially in the form of the 'Saturday to Monday' (the expression 'weekend' was considered vulgar in Victorian and Edwardian days).

At country stations all over the British Isles trains disgorged crowds of ladies and gentlemen from first class compartments, valets and lady's maids from third class compartments, leather trunks and (in the days of the late Victorian bicycling craze) bicycles from the luggage van. All were conveyed in fleets of carriages (for the gentry) and 'brakes' (for the servants) to neighbouring country houses to spend two or three days, or sometimes two or three weeks together. House parties were not necessarily held just for pleasure. They could be a way of pushing social or political ambitions, or putting one's daughters in company with eligible young men. Their make-up was as carefully worked out as the make-up of a dinner-party, and the names of the guests were listed in the social columns of the London newspapers. To have thirty or forty house guests was nothing out of the ordinary in a big country house.

Much of our knowledge of country houses comes from the letters or diaries written by guests. To have the freedom of a big house set in several square miles of woods and parkland, to share it with congenial company, to hunt, shoot, fish, gossip, argue, sightsee, flirt or play games together, could add up to one of the pleasantest ways of passing time ever devised. But the ideal was not always attained; some house parties were more an affair of rich people eating too much and being bored together in the rain. Some guests were uninvited or unwillingly invited; some were more censorious or difficult than others.

LOOKING AFTER GUESTS

THEN it must be seen if strangers shall be brought to chamber, and that the chamber be cleanly apparelled and dressed according to the time of year, as in winter time fire, in summer time the bed covered with pillows and head-sheets in case that they will rest. And after this done, they must have cheer of novelties in the chamber, as junket, cherries, pippins and such novelties as the time of year requireth; or else green ginger comfits, with such things as winter requireth; and sweet wines, as hippocras, tyre, muscadell, bastard, vernage, of the best that may be had, to the honour and laud of the principal of the house.

'FOR TO SERVE A LORD', FROM A MANUSCRIPT OF C. 1450–1500.

TROUBLE-SOME GUESTS AT HACKNESS 1600

ON Tuesday the 26th Aug. Sir Thomas Hoby was standing in his hall at Hackness, when there came in Sir W. Eure's foot-boy and said that his master and sundry other gentlemen would come that night. Sir Thomas answered that he was sorry, his wife was ill and he not so well provided for them as he wished, and desiring the footboy to tell his master as much, he answered that his master was hunting in the forest of Pickering Lyth, so as he knew not where to find him.

About two hours after, the above-named, Mr. Dawnay excepted, came to Hackness with sundry other servants and boys, and Sir Thomas hearing they were come into his dining-room went to them and told them they were welcome. Presently after this Sir William Eure's footboy took forth cards and laid them on the table, wherewith some of the gentlemen were exercised until supper. In the beginning of supper, Mr. Eure pretending he had come to hunt, Sir Thomas sent for his servant that had charge of his deer, who dwelt three miles from him, to come the next morning, and so continued with them all the time at supper, which was spent by the gentlemen partly in discoursing of horses and dogs, sports whereunto Sir Thomas never applied himself, partly with lascivious talk where every sentence was begun or ended with a

(left) A frisky horse: an incident when staying with Mr and Mrs Snow, Langton Lodge, Dorset. Diana Sperling, 1823.

great oath, and partly in inordinate drinking unto healths, abuses never practised by Sir Thomas.

In supper time came in a footboy whom they had sent for Mr. Dawnay, and brought word he would come in the morning. After supper Sir Thomas willed to have their chambers made ready, and came himself to bring them to their lodgings, but they being at dice told him they would play awhile, so he did leave them and went down and set his household to prayers as they were accustomed. When Sir Thomas and his family had begun to sing a psalm, the company above made an extraordinary noise with their feet, and some of them stood upon the stairs at a window opening into the hall, and laughed all the time to prayers.

The next morning they went to breakfast in the dining-room, and Sir Thomas hearing them call for more wine, sent for the key of the cellar and told them·they should come by no more wine from him. Presently Sir Thomas sent to Mr. Eure to know how he would bestow that day, and told him if he would leave disquieting him with carding, dicing and excessive drinking, and fall to other sports, they should be very welcome. After this message Mr. Eure sent to Sir Thomas's wife that he would see her and begone, whereunto she answered she was in bed and when she was ready she would send him word.

At his coming she prayed him to depart the house in quietness, and going to the rest of the company, he called a servant of Sir Thomas, and said 'Tell thy master he hath sent me scurvy messages, and the next time I meet him I will tell him so, if he be upon the bench, and will pull him by the beard.' Coming to the uttermost court, Mr Eure said he would go to the top of the hill and fling down mill-stones ... at the same time throwing stones at the windows and breaking four quarrels of glass.

Hatfield MSS

VISITING

IN

CORNWALL

1602

ALL Cornish gentlemen are cousins ... They converse familiarly together, and often visit one another. A gentleman and his wife will ride to make merry with his next neighbour, and after a day or twain those two couples go to a third, in which progress they increase like snowballs, till through their burdensome weight they break again.

RICHARD CAREW, *The Survey of Cornwall*

48

LORD

GUILDFORD'S

BROTHER

MEETS

THE

ALDERMEN

AT

WROXTON

ABBEY

1684

BUT after dinner in came my old acquaintance the mayor and aldermen, with the council of the neighbour corporation of Banbury. And my brother came out to them and received their compliment, and having answered and drank to them retired to his better company, and left them to me in charge to make welcome. I thought that sack was the business and drunkenness the end, and the sooner over the better; so I ordered two servants to attend us with salvers, glasses and bottles, and not to leave us wherever we went. Then I plied them sitting, standing, walking in all places with the creatures (for I walked them all over the house to shew the rooms and buildings, and sometimes we sat and sometimes stood) until I had finished the work, took leave and dismissed them to their lodgings in ditches homeward bound. But having had a load at dinner, which made me so valiant in this attack, and such a surcharge after, it proved not only a crapula but a surfeit. And I made my way like a wounded deer to a shady moist place, and laid me down all on fire as I thought myself upon the ground; and there evaporated for four or five hours, and then rose very sick, and scarce recovered in some days.

ROGER NORTH, *Lives of the Norths*

THE

PLEASURES

OF

CIRENCESTER

1718

IT is the place that of all others I fancy . . . I write an hour or two every morning, then ride out a hunting upon the Downs, eat heartily, talk tender sentiments with Lord Bathurst, or draw plans for houses and gardens, open avenues, cut glades, plant firs, contrive water-works, all very fine and beautiful in our own imagination. At night we play at commerce and play pretty high: I do more, I bet too; for I am really rich, and must throw away my money if no deserving friend will use it. I like this course of life so well that I am resolved to stay here till I hear of somebody's being in town that is worth coming after.

ALEXANDER POPE TO THE MISSES BLOUNT, CIRENCESTER PARK, GLOUCESTERSHIRE, 8 OCTOBER, 1718

. . . AND OF STOWE 1739

This garden is beyond all description in the new part of it. I am every hour in it, but dinner and night, and every hour envying myself the delight of it. . . . Every one takes a different way, and wanders about till we meet at noon. All the mornings we breakfast and dispute; after dinner, and at night, music and harmony; in the garden, fishing; no politics and no cards, nor much reading. This agrees exactly with me; for the want of cards sends us early to bed. I have no complaints, but that I wish for you and cannot have you.

ALEXANDER POPE TO THE MISSES BLOUNT, STOWE,
BUCKINGHAMSHIRE, 4 JULY, 1739.

Henry Fox and his friends, perhaps in the garden at Water Eaton House, Oxfordshire. William Hogarth, c. 1738.

POPE

CONDOLES

WITH

TERESA

BLOUNT

ON

A

COUNTRY

VISIT

1714

SHE went to plain work, and to purling brooks,
Old fashion'd halls, dull aunts, and croaking rooks:
She went from opera, park, assembly, play,
To morning walks, and prayers three hours a day;
To part her time 'twixt reading and bohea,
To muse, and spill her solitary tea,
Or o'er cold coffee trifle with the spoon,
Count the slow clock, and dine exact at noon;
Divert her eyes with pictures in the fire,
Hum half a tune, tell stories to the squire;
Up to her godly garret after seven,
There starve and pray, for that's the way to heaven.
  Some squire, perhaps, you take delight to rack,
Whose game is whisk, whose treat a toast in sack;
Who visits with a gun, presents you birds,
Then gives a smacking buss, and cries – no words;
Or with his hounds comes hallooing from the stable,
Makes love with nods, and knees beneath a table;
Whose laughs are hearty, though his jests are coarse,
And loves you best of all things – but his horse.

From ALEXANDER POPE, TO A YOUNG LADY, ON HER LEAVING
THE TOWN AFTER THE CORONATION, 1714

SIR

ROBERT

WALPOLE

ENTERTAINS

FRIENDS

AND

NEIGHBOURS

AT

HIS

BIANNUAL

'CONGRESS'

AT

HOUGHTON

1731

THE base, or rustic story, is what is chiefly inhabited at the Congress. There is a room for breakfast, another for supper, another for dinner, another for afternooning, and the great arcade with four chimneys for walking and quid-nuncing. The rest of this floor is merely for use, by which your Royal Highness must perceive that the whole is dedicated to fox-hunters, hospitality, noise, dirt and business ... We have a whole house full of people, but every body does so much what he pleases, that one's next room neighbour is no more trouble to one here than one's next door neighbour in London ...

Our company swelled at last into so numerous a body that we used to sit down to dinner a little snug party of about thirty odd, up to the chin in beef, venison, geese, turkeys, etc.; and generally over the chin in claret, strong beer and punch. We had Lords spiritual and temporal, besides commoners, parsons and freeholders innumerable. In public we drank loyal healths, talked of the times, and cultivated popularity; in private we drew plans and cultivated the country.

LORD HERVEY TO FREDERICK, PRINCE OF WALES,
HOUGHTON HALL, NORFOLK, 14, 16, AND 21 JULY, 1731

LORD

BYRON'S

HOUSE-

PARTY

AT

NEWSTEAD

ABBEY

1809

OUR party consisted of Lord Byron and four others, and was, now and then, increased by the presence of a neighbouring parson. As for our way of living, the order of the day was generally this:- for breakfast we had no set hour, but each suited his own convenience, – every thing remaining on the table till the whole party had done; though had one wished to breakfast at the early hour of ten, we would have been rather lucky to find any of the servants up. Our average hour of rising

was one. I, who generally got up between eleven and twelve, was always, – even when an invalid, – the first of the party, and was esteemed a prodigy of early rising. It was frequently past two before the breakfast party broke up. Then, for the amusements of the morning, there was reading, fencing, single-stick, or shuttlecock, in the great room; practising with pistols in the hall; walking – riding – cricket – sailing on the lake, playing with the bear, or teasing the wolf. Between seven and eight we dined; and our evening lasted from that time till one, two, or three in the morning. The evening diversions may be easily conceived.

I must not omit the custom of handing round, after dinner, on the removal of the cloth, a human skull filled with burgundy. After revelling on choice viands, and the finest wines of France, we adjourned to tea, where we amused ourselves with reading, or improving conversation, – each, according to his fancy, – and, after sandwiches, etc., retired to rest. A set of monkish dresses, which had been provided, with all the proper apparatus of crosses, beads, tonsures, etc., often gave a variety of our appearance, and to our pursuits.

C.S. MATTHEWS TO HIS SISTER, 22 MAY, 1809

An artist painting at Petworth, c. 1828, sketched by J.M.W. Turner when a fellow guest.

TODAY, for instance, I observed the company was distributed in the following manner. Our suffering host lay on the sofa, dozing a little; five ladies and gentlemen were very attentively reading in various sorts of books (of this number I was one, having some views of parks before me); another had been playing for a quarter of an hour with a long-suffering dog; two old Members of Parliament were disputing vehemently about the 'Corn Bill'; and the rest of the company were in a dimly-lighted room adjoining, where a pretty girl was playing on the piano-forte, and another with a most perforating voice, singing ballads.

... A light supper of cold meats and fruits is brought, at which everyone helps himself, and shortly after midnight all retire. A number of small candlesticks stand ready on a side-table; every man takes his own, and lights himself up to bed; for the greater part of the servants, who have to rise early, are, as is fair and reasonable, gone to bed.

PRINCE PÜCKLER-MUSKAU, *Tour*

AS far as tobacco is concerned it is said that the Duke of Wellington would only allow smoking in his house after the ladies had retired to bed. He would then inform the gentlemen that those who wished to indulge in the objectionable pastime could do so in the Servant's Hall.

JOHN JAMES, *Memoirs of a House Steward*

Edward Lear's impression of himself sketching at Nuneham Park, Oxfordshire, c. 1860.

SWINBURNE

READS

HIS

POEMS

AT

FRYSTON

1863

... IN April of that year Lady Ritchie recalls for me that the Houghtons stimulated the curiosity of their guests by describing the young poet who was to arrive later. She was in the garden on the afternoon of his arrival, and she saw him advance up the sloping lawn swinging his hat in his hand, and letting the sunshine flood the bush of his red-gold hair. He looked like Apollo or a fairy prince ... On Sunday evening after dinner he was asked to read some of his poems. His choice was injudicious; he is believed to have recited *The Leper*; it is certain that he read *Les Noyades*! At this the Archbishop of York made so shocked a face that Thackeray smiled and whispered to Lord Houghton, while the two young ladies, who had never heard such sentiments expressed before, giggled aloud. Their laughter offended the poet, who, however, was soothed by Lady Houghton ... *Les Noyades* was then proceeding on its amazing course, and the Archbishop was looking more and more horrified when suddenly the butler – 'like an avenging angel', as Lady Ritchie says – threw open the door and announced 'Prayers, my Lord!'

EDMUND GOSSE, *Swinburne*

HENRY

JAMES

STAYS

WITH

THE

PORTS-

MOUTHS

1878

I am paying a short visit at what I suppose is called here a 'great house', viz. at Lord Portsmouth's. Lady P., whom I met last summer at Wenlock Abbey, & who is an extremely nice woman, asked me a great while since to come here at this point, for a week. I accepted for three days, two of which have happily expired – for when the moment came I was very indisposed to leave London. That is the worst of invitations given you so long in advance, when the time comes you are apt to be not at all in the same humour as when they were accepted. ...

The place and country are of course very beautiful & Lady P. 'most kind'; but though there are several people in the house (local gentlefolk, of no distinctive qualities) the whole thing is dull. This is a large family, chiefly of infantine sons and daughters (there are 12!) who live in some mysterious part of the house & are never seen. The one chiefly about is young Lord Lymington, the eldest son, an aimiable youth of 21, attended by a pleasant young Oxford man, with whom he is 'reading'. Lord P. is simply a great hunting and racing magnate, who keeps the hounds in this part of the country, and is absent all day with them. There is nothing in the house but pictures of horses – and awfully bad ones at that.

The life is very simple and tranquil. Yesterday, before lunch, I walked in the garden with Lady Rosamund, who is not 'out' & doesn't dine at table, though she is a very pretty little pink and white creature of 17; & in the p.m. Lady P. showed me her boudoir which she is 'doing up', with old china &c.; & then took me to drive in her phaeton, through some lovely Devonshire lanes. In the evening we had a 'ballet'; i.e. the little girls, out of the schoolroom, came down into the gallery, with their governess, & danced cachuckas, minuets, &c. with the utmost docility & modesty, while we sat about & applauded.

To-day is bad weather, & I am sitting alone in a big cold library, of totally unread books, waiting for Lord Portsmouth, who has offered to take me out & show me his stables & kennels (famous ones), to turn up. I shall try & get away tomorrow, which is a Saturday; as I don't think I could stick out a Sunday here ... It may interest you [to] know, as a piece of local color that, though there are six or seven resident flunkeys here, I have been trying in vain, for the last half hour, to get the expiring fire refreshed. Two or three of them have been in to look at it – but it appears to be no-one's business to bring in coals ...

I have come to my room to dress for dinner, in obedience to the bell, which is just being tolled. A footman in blue & silver has just come in to 'put out' my things – he almost poured out the quantum of water I am to wash by. The visit to the stables was deferred till after lunch, when I went the rounds with Lord P. and a couple of men who were staying here – 40 horses, mostly hunters, & a wonderful pack of foxhounds – lodged like superior mechanics!

HENRY JAMES TO HIS FATHER, EGGESFORD HOUSE, NORTH DEVON, OCTOBER 18, 1878

MR

COBDEN-

SANDERSON

LEAVES

NAWORTH

CASTLE

1892

A row blew up between my mother and Cobden-Sanderson, which (as I learnt long after) arose from a stormy argument on whether or not the middle class were 'all snobs' and aristocrats 'unsurpassingly charming'. Both were furious, both were insulting. She 'turned him out of the house', he 'would not stay under her roof another hour'. Not even in a time of desperate anxiety [his children had bad influenza] would either of these fiery fighters make allowance for each other's hot temper. Cobden-Sanderson took himself off to an

Detail from a photograph of a shooting party at Blenheim, 1896. The Prince and Princess of Wales seated, A.J. Balfour 3rd from the left in the back row.

inn in the little town of Brampton, leaving his boy and girl to be looked after in the harassed castle. Every morning he got a Brampton fly to drive him over to Naworth. He stood for some twenty minutes in the courtyard signalling and gesticulating to the window where his children were ill. He was a tiny little man, dressed in a pinkish Norfolk jacket and knickerbockers, with thin little legs in black stockings, and a deer-stalker cap. It was a fascinating sight – and when by child-magic we knew the show was ready, we watched it from a window. That was the last of the Cobden-Sandersons; but his version of the story is too good to leave out. My mother, he said, having ordered him out of the house on the spot, and the children being too ill to move, my mother refused to feed them. So every day a basket was lowered to the courtyard from their high-up bedroom window, and he put food that he had brought from Brampton into it for them.

DOROTHY HENLEY, *Rosalind Howard Countess of Carlisle*

MR BALFOUR IS BLASÉ AT BLENHEIM 1896

THERE is here a big party in a big house at a big park beside a big lake. To begin with . . . 'the Prince of Wales and the rest of the Royal family –' or if not that, at least a quorum, namely himself, his wife, 2 daughters and a son-in-law. There are two sets of George Curzons, the Londonderrys, Grenfells, Gosfords, H. Chaplin, etc. etc. We came down by special train – rather cross most of us – were received with illuminations, guards of honour, cheering and other follies, went through agonies about our luggage, but finally settled down placidly enough.

Today the men shot and the women dawdled. As I detest both occupations equally, I stayed in my room till one o'clock and then went exploring on my bike, joining everybody at luncheon. Then again after the inevitable photograph, I again betook myself to my faithful machine and here I am writing to you. So far you perceive the duties of society are weighing lightly upon me.

LETTER FROM A. J. BALFOUR TO LADY ELCHO, 1896

A ROUGH AWAKENING AT CHATSWORTH C. 1900

THE Ante-Room. This was the telephone room when the only telephone was in a sort of shrine. In spite of the size of the house it was not unknown to lodge a male guest here when there was a big party. In the Eighth Duke's time a friend of the Duke of Portland's slept here on a camp bed and was much amused when early in the morning the letter bags were thrown on top of him and the postman shouted, 'Get up you lazy devil, you've overslept again!'

DEBORAH, DUCHESS OF DEVONSHIRE, *The House*

RAYMOND ASQUITH TAKES AGAINST CHATSWORTH 1906

HOW you would loathe this place! It crushes one by its size and is full of smart shrivelled up people. Lady Helen Vincent is the only beauty here and Lady Theo Acheson the only girl – quite nice but not very interesting. I have been a long walk with her in the snow this afternoon – sometimes up to our waists: but I never found it necessary to lift her out of a drift. There is some very mild tobogganing and a good deal of bridge, but shooting and skating are prevented by the snow, and there is only *one* bathroom in the house, which is kept for the King.

RAYMOND ASQUITH TO KATHERINE HORNER, CHATSWORTH, 29 DECEMBER, 1906

. . . . AND ENJOYS (ON THE WHOLE) CLOVELLY, 1901

I am so sorry when I think of you at Brighton and myself here that I cannot help writing to you, though in a few hours from now – damnably few – I shall be lifting my aching bones from a couch which has hardly had time to take the impress of my body and preparing for the great adventure of the day. For it is the custom of the house to plunge *en échelon* into the Atlantic Ocean as near the centre of it as may be at precisely 5 minutes before 8 every morning. We are rowed out in purple bathing dresses by bronzed descendants of Armada heroes

until there is no land in sight but the Island of Lundy and then at a given signal we leap into the blue and bottomless swell and are borne hither and thither like helpless jelly fish in the racing tide.

Having sustained ourselves in the waves so long as our strength holds out we crawl again into the boats and are ferried back to a great lugger anchored off the harbour mouth where we find our clothes elegantly disposed by careful valets; we cover our bodies; light cigarettes and are taken back to land where we find a herd of black thoroughbred Dartmoor ponies; each man and woman selects a mount and we clamber up a sheer precipice where the occasional ash give a perilous foothold and so over a rolling park back to the house where we are welcomed by a smoking mass of lobsters and great dishes of honey and Devonshire cream.

It is a curious life, and being a poor swimmer I find it a little tiring – But the place is so beautiful as to repay any fatigues imposed on one by a barbarous tradition. It really is so marvellously beautiful that description is impotent. If you can imagine the softer glories of an Italian lake crowned by a clean Greek sky and the strong northern air which has fed our Drakes and Hawkins', our Jervises, Collingwoods and Rodneys for countless generations – crimson cliffs thickly mantled with oaks and rhododendrons sliding into a cerulean sea – you have some faint idea of the place. Add to this a square white house standing 400 feet above the sea in a park dappled with fallow-deer, surrounded by smooth lawns and dewy terraces glistening with sun-dials of Parian marble, great trees and luscious shrubs and red garden walls glowing with peaches and nectarines, and shade so cunningly arranged that you can be cool at mid-day and hot in the setting sun and you will admit that Brighton cannot equal it.

The cook is good, the wines are good, the servants are good; at ¼ past 7 every morning a handsome rascal in red plush breeches lays by one's bedside a plate of raspberries and a glass of milk with 6 drops of brandy in it to fortify one for the sea, and large flagons of icy cup are alluringly disposed throughout the day in the mossy shadows of ancient beeches. In the morning one reads at length on cushions in the bright air and in the afternoon we shoot deer and rabbits in the bracken or pull in mackerel from the decks of red sailed boats . . .

RAYMOND ASQUITH TO H.T. BAKER, CLOVELLY COURT, DEVON, 1 AUGUST, 1901

House-party on ice at Eastwell Park, Kent, c. 1860

GARSINGTON:
DAVID
GARNETT
REMEMBERS
1955

GARSINGTON was on the slope of a hill. The approach was down a lane with farm buildings on the right hand side, screening it, so that the lovely dignified front of the Tudor Manor House came as a surprise. It was noble, even grand, yet it was the very reverse of ostentatious.

Inside there were several large panelled rooms, which had, I surmise, been a mixture of genuine seventeenth-century and Victorian baronial styles before Ottoline [Morrell] descended upon them. She had transformed them, stamping her personality ruthlessly everywhere. The oak panelling had been painted a dark peacock blue-green; the bare and sombre dignity of Elizabethan wood and stone had been overwhelmed with an almost oriental magnificence: the luxuries of silk curtains and Persian carpets, cushions and pouffes. Ottoline's pack of pug dogs trotted everywhere and added to the Beardsley quality, which was one half of her natural taste. The characteristic of every house in which Ottoline lived was its smell and the smell of Garsington was stronger than that of Bedford Square. It reeked of the bowls of pot-pourri and orris-root which stood on every mantelpiece, side table and windowsill and of the desiccated oranges, studded with cloves, which Ottoline loved making. The walls were covered with a variety of pictures. Italian pictures and bric-à-brac, drawings by John, water-colours for fans by Conder, who was rumoured to have been one of Ottoline's first conquests, paintings by Duncan and Gertler and a dozen other of the younger artists.

Greeting us was Philip Morrell in riding breeches and rat-catcher coat with a glassy geniality gleaming in his eyes and his head thrown so far back that the high bridge of his nose was level with his forehead. And the pugs barked their welcome.

DAVID GARNETT *The Flowers of the Forest*

GUESTS REACT, 1916–19.
I came here with the notion of working. Mon Dieu! There are now no intervals between the weekends – the flux and reflux is endless – and I sit quivering among a surging mess of pugs, peacocks, pianolas, and humans – if humans they can be called – the inhabitants of this Circe's cave. I am now faced not only with Carrington and Brett

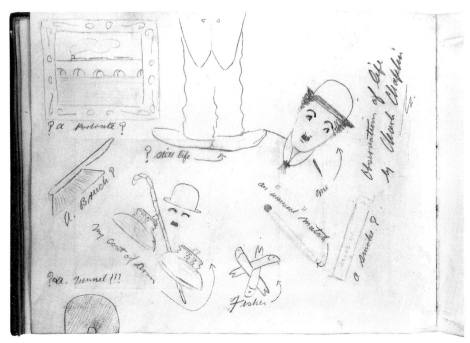

(more or less permanencies now) but Gertler, who . . . is at the present moment carolling a rag-time in union with her Ladyship. I feel like an open boat in a choppy sea – but thank goodness the harbour is in sight.

LYTTON STRACHEY TO BARBARA HILES, 17 JULY, 1916

KATHERINE MANSFIELD WRITES A THANK-YOU NOTE
My memory of the days we had spent together was as perfect as ever – as bright as untroubled. I still saw the blue spears of lavender – the trays of fading scented leaves, you in your room, and your bed with the big white pillow – and you coming down in the garden swinging the gay lantern.

KATHERINE MANSFIELD TO OTTOLINE MORRELL,
11 AUGUST 1917

VIRGINIA WOOLF WRITES TO OTTOLINE
Katherine Mansfield describes your garden, the rose leaves drying in the sun, the pool, and long conversations between people wandering up and down in the moonlight.

VIRGINIA WOOLF TO OTTOLINE MORRELL, 15 AUGUST, 1917

VIRGINIA WRITES TO HER SISTER
The worst of a weekend on that scale is that one gets rather stupefied before it is over. I had a private talk with Ott: and on the whole I think that she has been slightly maligned. At least she was more vivacious and malicious and less vapourish than I expected . . . There were endless young men from Oxford, and Brett and Lytton and Aldous Huxley who talks too much about his prose romances for my taste, and falls into deep gloom when, according to Ott: he is thinking of Maria.

VIRGINIA WOOLF TO VANESSA BELL, 27 NOVEMBER, 1917

VIRGINIA WRITES TO JANET CARE
. . . after two days of it, the discomfort is considerably worse than mere boredom. There are, of course, visits by night to ones bedroom; and then if one can't come up to the scratch the poor old creature gets more and more harassed and desperate; her paint runs too, and her powder blows off . . .

VIRGINIA WOOLF TO JANET CARE, JULY 23, 1919

ONE DUCHESS TEASES ANOTHER C. 1920

THE winter shooting parties and Christmas were the busiest time at Chatsworth. Every November the Duke and Duchess of Portland came over from Welbeck for four or five days' pheasant shooting. Although the two duchesses were friends there was some rivalry between them over their houses and the things in them. For these parties a great display of gold and

60

Charlie Chaplin's signature in Sir Philip Sassoon's visitors' book, Port Lympne, Kent.

silver was put on in the dining room. Winnie Portland, well aware that every piece was out on show, used to tease Evie Devonshire by waiting for a pause in the conversation and saying, 'Evie, will you take us down to the strongroom after dinner and show us the plate?'

DEBORAH, DUCHESS OF DEVONSHIRE *The House*

A HOUSE-PARTY AT RENISHAW 1930

WENT to Renishaw. Travelled down with Robert [Byron] who made me go third class. He says he only travels first class abroad because he thinks it is expected of Englishmen. We arrived at Chesterfield Station and found Sachie and Georgia [Sitwell] there to meet us. Also Willie Walton, Harold Monro, a young man, very mad and conceited, called Gaspard Ponsonby (son of Fritz). At Renishaw we found Francis Birrell, Arthur Waley, a nasty man called Roderick and the entire family.

Renishaw very large and rather forbidding. Arterial main roads, coal mines, squalid industrial village, then a park, partly laid out as a golf course, and the house; north front, discoloured Derbyshire stone, castellated. Very dark hall. Many other rooms of great beauty, fine tapestry and Italian furniture. Ginger [Sir George Sitwell] in white tie and tail coat very gentle. Ginger and Lady Ida never allowed to appear together at meals. The house extremely noisy owing to shunting all round it. The lake black with coal dust. A finely laid out terrace garden with a prospect of undulating hills, water and the pit-heads, slag heaps and factory chimneys.

Georgia exquisitely dressed among all these shabby men. G.P. in love with her. She got very much stouter during the ten days I was there chiefly because of bathing and the very good food (chef from Ritz) about which all the family complained. Most of the party left after the weekend. Robert shut himself in his bedroom most of the day. Later Ankaret and William Jackson arrived. I summoned Alastair who had returned to England. The household was very full of plots. Almost everything was a secret and most of the conversations deliberately engineered in prosecution of some private joke. Ginger, for instance, was told

that Ankaret's two subjects were Arctic exploration and ecclesiastical instruments; also that Alastair played the violin. Sachie liked talking about sex. Osbert very shy. Edith wholly ignorant. We talked of slums. She said the poor streets of Scarborough are terrible but that she did not think that the fishermen took drugs very much. She also said that port was made with methylated spirit; she knew this for a fact because her charwoman told her.

The servants very curious. They live on terms of feudal familiarity. E.g., a message brought by footman to assembled family that her ladyship wanted to see Miss Edith upstairs. 'I can't go. I've been with her all day. Osbert, you go.' 'Sachie, you go.' 'Georgia, you go', etc. Footman: 'Well, come on. One of you's got to go.' Osbert's breakfast was large slices of pineapple and melon. No one else was allowed these. Osbert kept cigars and smoked them secretly. I brought my own. The recreations of the household were bathing, visiting houses, and Osbert's Walk. We went to Hardwick – a vilely ugly house but full of good needlework. Osbert's Walk consisted of driving in the car a quarter of a mile to Eckington Woods, walking through them, about half an hour (with bracken), the car meeting him on the other side

and taking him home. He did this every day. There was a golf club where we had morning drinks. This too was a secret. Georgia is the centre of all the plots.

EVELYN WAUGH, *Diaries* 1930

A HOUSE-PARTY AT CLIVEDEN 1930

DOWN to Cliveden. A dark autumnal day. Thirty-two people in the house. Cold and draughty. Great sofas in vast cathedrals: little groups of people wishing they were alone: a lack of organisation and occupation: a desultory drivel. The party is in itself good enough. Duff and Diana [Cooper], Tom Mosley and Cimmie. Oliver Stanley and Lady Maureen, Harold Macmillan and Lady Dorothy, Bracken, Garvin, Bob Boothby, Malcolm Bullock. But it does not hang together. After dinner, in order to enliven the party, Lady Astor dons a Victorian hat and a pair of false teeth. It does not enliven the party.

Diary of Harold Nicolson, 29 November, 1930

Family and guests at Madresfield Court, Worcestershire, in the 1920s. (Left to right) Evelyn Waugh, Hamish Erskine, Dorothy Lygon, Hubert Duggan.
(right) Menu card, Wilden House, 17 January, 1879.

WILDEN
JANUARY 15 1879

Mock Turtle Soup.
Turbet with Lobster Sauce.
Oyster Patés.
Stewed Kidneys.
Boiled Turkey – Tongue with Oyster Sauce.
Roast Haunch of Mutton
Pheasants à la Gitana.
Roast Hare.
Plum Pudding.
Mince Pies.
Jellies &c. Cheesecakes &c.

4
Eating
&
Drinking

*F*ood and drink had a symbolic role in country houses. To consume it, or cause others to consume it, in enormous quantities suggested power, wealth and hospitality at one go. From the Middle Ages onwards the hecatombs that vanished down the throats of guests at feasts and funerals were carefully recorded.

It was a sign of status for an individual to be served more food than he or she could conceivably eat. In the Middle Ages food came up in what were called 'messes'; each mess contained the same amount of food, but could be served to one great man or six or more lesser persons. The former ate what he felt like; what was left over was passed down the hierarchy until the final remnants reached the beggars at the gate. Consuelo, Duchess of Marlborough, records how this medieval procedure was still lingering on at Blenheim in the 1890s. The vast spreads at country-house breakfasts, as described by Harold Nicolson, were an example of conspicuous waste adapted for Edwardian life.

The route taken by food was part of the symbolism. Serving up a meal became a ritual. The distance between kitchen to dining room was often vast, through deliberate choice rather than bad planning: it allowed for a grand procession, and reduced smells and danger of fire. To want the food to be hot seems to have been a nineteenth-century refinement. Appearance was perhaps more important than taste; certainly, care was lavished on the visual conceits which diversified great feasts, and were the predecessors of the fancy wedding cakes of today.

It can be a relief to move from the orgies being prepared in the kitchen to the refinements of the still room. The stills known as alembics were the equivalent of microwave cookers in the late sixteenth and early seventeenth centuries: new toys with which the mistress of the house personally distilled cordials, medicines and toilet waters. Other forms of medicine were also prepared in the still room, along with dessert delicacies which were the ancestors of the cakes, preserves and biscuits which furnished Edwardian tea-tables.

By then, however, the still room had long since been taken over by the housekeeper. In the late eighteenth and nineteenth centuries the dairy was the place where the mistress of the house amused herself. It was on show to guests who would never have thought of penetrating to the kitchen. Dairy maids could go far. Lady Fetherstonhaugh, the owner of the great house of Uppark in Sussex in the late nineteenth century, had started life as one, her buxom arms busy at the churn catching the fancy of her baronet employer.

Medieval cooks, from the *Luttrell Psalter*.

Col. Pl. V William Brooke, 10th Lord Cobham and his family. Unidentified artist, 1567.

Col. Pl. VI (following page top) The Sperling family at dinner at Dynes Hall, Essex. Diana Sperling, c.1812–13.

Col. Pl. VII (following page bottom) A tea-party at St Fagan's. Detail from the painting of Lord and Lady Windsor and family by Sir John Lavery, 1905.

WEDDING FOOD IN THE FIFTEENTH CENTURY

FOR TO MAKE A FEAST FOR A BRIDE

The first course

Brawn with the boar's head, lying in a field, edged about with
a scripture saying in this wise:

> Welcome you brethren goodly in this hall
> Joy be unto you all
> That on this day it is now fall.
> That worthy lord that lay in an ox stall
> Maintain your husband and you, with your guests all.

Frumenty with venison, swan, pig, pheasant, with a great custard,
with a subtilty: a lamb standing in scripture, saying in this wise:

> I meekly unto you, sovereign, am sent
> To dwell with you and ever be present.

The second course

Venison in broth, viand Ryalle, venison roasted, crane, cony,
a baked meat, leche damask, with a subtilty: an antelope sitting
on a selc that sayeth with scripture:

> Be-eth all glad and merry that sitteth at this mess,
> And prayeth for the king and all his.

The third course

Cream of almonds, losynge in syrup, bittern, partridge, plover,
snipe, powder veal, leche veal, whelks in subtilty, roches in subtilty,
place in subtilty: a baked meat with a subtilty: an angel with a
scripture:

> Thank all, God, of this feast.

The fourth course

Payne puff, cheese freynes, bread hot, with a cake, and a wife lying
in child-bed, with a scripture saying in this wise:

> I am coming toward your bride
> If ye durst once look to me ward
> I ween you needs must.

Another course or service
Brawn with mustard, umblys of a deer or of a sheep; swan, capon,
lamb.

DAVENPORT MSS

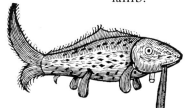

HINTS

FROM

THE

COUNTESS

OF

KENT

1653

AGAINST melancholy. Take one spoonful of gilliflowers, the weight of seven barley corns of Bezer-stone, bruise it as fine as flour, and so put it into two spoonfuls of syrup of gilliflowers, and take it four hours after dinner, this will cheer the heart.

To take away a hoarseness. Take a turnip, cut a hole in the top of it, and fill it up with brown sugar-candy, and so roast it in the embers, and eat it with butter.

To take away the head-ache. Take the best salad oil, and the glass half full with the tops of poppy flowers which groweth in the corn, set this in the sun a fortnight, and so keep it all the year, and anoint the temples of your head with it.

For a cough. Take salad oil, *Aqua vitae*, and sack, of each in equal quantity, heat them altogether, and before the fire rub the soles of your feet with it.

THE COUNTESS OF KENT'S *Choice Manual*

THE

COUNTESS

OF

DORSET'S

RECIPE

FOR

WHITE

METHEGLIN

1668

TAKE Rosemary, Thyme, Sweet-bryar, Penny-royal, Bays, Water-cresses, Agrimony, Marshmallow leaves, Liver-wort, Maiden-hair, Betony, Eyebright, Scabious, the bark of the Ash-tree, Eringoroots, Green-wild-Angelica, Ribwort, Sanicle, Roman-worm-wood, Tamarisk, Mother-thyme, Sassafras, Philipendula, of each of these herbs a like proportion; or of as many of them as you please to put in. But you must put in all but four handfuls of herbs, which you must steep one night, and one day, in a little bowl of water, being close covered; the next day take another quantity of fresh water, and boil the same herbs in it, till the colour be very high; then take another quantity of water, and boil the same herbs in it, until they look green; and so let it boil three or four times in several waters, as long as the Liquor looketh any thing green.

Then let it stand with these herbs in it a day and night. Remember the last water you boil it in to the proportion of herbs, must be twelve gallons of water, and when it hath stood a day and a night, with these herbs in it, after the last boiling, then strain the Liquor from the herbs, and put as much of the finest and best honey into the Liquor, as will make it bear an Egg. You must work and labour the honey and liquor together one whole day, until the honey be consumed.

Then let it stand a whole night, and then let it be well laboured again, and let it stand again a clearing, and so boil it again a quarter of an hour, with the whites of six New-laid-eggs with the shells, the yolks being taken out; so scum it very clean, and let it stand a day a cooling. Then put it into a barrel, and take Cloves, Mace, Cinnamon, and Nutmegs, as much as will please your taste, and beat them altogether; put them into a linen bag, and hang it with a thread in the barrel. Take heed you put not too much spice in; a little will serve. Take the whites of two or three New-laid-eggs, a spoonful of balm, and a spoonful of Wheat-flower, and beat them altogether, and put it into your Liquor into the barrel, and let it work, before you stop it.

Then afterwards stop it well, and close it well with clay and Salt tempered together, and let it be set in a close place; and when it hath been settled some six weeks, draw it into bottles, and stop it very close, and drink it not a month after: but it will keep well half a year, and more.

The Closet of Sir Kenelm Digby

FANCY

COOKING

FOR

CHRISTMAS

AND

FEASTS

1660

MAKE the likeness of a Ship in Paste-board, with Flags and Streamers, the Guns belonging to it of Kickses [kickshaws], bind them about with pack-thread, and cover them with close paste proportionable to the fashion of a Cannon with Carriages, lay them in places convenient as you see them in Ships of war, with such holes and trains of powder that they may all take fire; Place your Ship firm in the great Charger; then make a salt round about it, and stick therein eggshells full of sweet water, you may by a great Pin take all the meat out of the egg by blowing, and then fill it up with the rose-water, then in another Charger have the proportion of a Stag made of coarse paste, with a broad Arrow in

To make a Pheasant *of a* Rabbit, *truss'd in such a manner, that it will appear like a* Pheasant, *and eat like one, with its Sauce. This is called, by the topping* Poulterers, *a* Poland-Chicken, *or a* Portugal-Chicken. *But it is most like a* Pheasant, *if it is larded. From Mrs.* Johnson, *at the famous* Eating-House *in* Devereux-Court *near the* Temple.

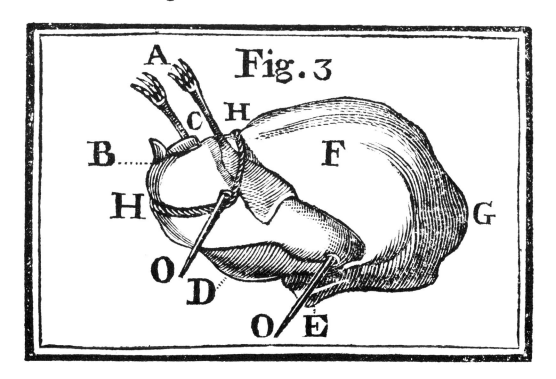

TAKE a young Rabbit full grown; case it all, excepting the Fore-Feet, chop

the side of him, and his body filled up with claret-wine; in another Charger at the end have the proportion of a Castle with Battlements, Portcullises, Gates and Draw-Bridges made of Pasteboard, the Guns and Kickses, and covered with coarse paste as the former; place it at a distance from the ship to fire at each other. The Stag being placed betwixt them with egg shells full of sweet water placed in salt.

At each side of the Charger wherein is the Stag, place a Pie made of coarse paste filled with bran, and yellowed over with saffron or the yolks of eggs, gild them over in spots, as also the Stag, the Ship, and Castle; bake them, and place them with gilt bay-leaves on turrets and tunnels of the Castle and Pies; being baked, make a hole in the bottom of your pies, take out the bran, put in your Frogs, and Birds, and close up the holes with the same coarse paste, then cut the Lids neatly up; To be taken off the Tunnels; being all placed in order upon the Table, before you fire the trains of powder, order it so that some of the Ladies may be persuaded to pluck the Arrow out of the Stag, then will the Claret-wine follow, as blood that runneth out of a wound.

This being done with admiration to the beholders, after some short pause, fire the train of the Castle, that the pieces all of one side may go off, then fire the Trains of one side of the Ship as in a battle; next turn the chargers; and by degrees fire the trains of each side as before. This done, to sweeten the stink of powder, let the Ladies take the egg shells full of sweet-waters and throw them at each other. All dangers being seemingly over, by this time you may suppose they will desire to see what is in the pies; where lifting first the lid off one pie, out skip some Frogs; which make the Ladies to skip and shriek; next after the other pie, whence come out the birds, who by a natural instinct flying in the light, will put out the Candles, so that what with the flying Birds and skipping Frogs, the one above, the other beneath, will cause much delight and pleasure to the whole company: at length the Candles are lighted, and a banquet brought in, the Music sounds, and every one with much delight and content rehearses their actions in the former passages. These were formerly the delights of the Nobility, before good Housekeeping had left *England*, and the Sword really acted that which was only counterfeited in such honest and laudable exercises as these.

ROBERT MAY, *The Accomplisht Cook*

A WEDDING MENU, 1683

A Bisque of Pigeons
A Sirloin of Beef Royal with Fillets Larded
A Pastry of Venison in Blood
Carps Curbouisson
Pigs darling with Olives of Veal larded
Hams and Tongues. Chi'nered Cold
Crayfish Pottage
Geese Roasted
A Patty Royal
A Haunch of Venison roasted, marinated with a neck of Veal

A fresh Salmon Colvert with marinated Fish
A Bisquet of Veal ragou'd
A Joale of Sturgeon marinated with other Fish
A Patty of Lumber with Trouts about it
Pickled Pullets in Jelly
6 legs of Lamb a la Daube
6 Lambs heads Larded and broiled
Potage de Sante

For ye Middle of ye Table

A square dish of sweet meats
2 dishes of China oranges with each 100

2 pyramids of Fruits
2 pryamids of Sweet meats

To Remove etc. 3 Pottage

1 chine of mutton and veal with Cutlets
a pike Roasted with other Fish about it
A Westphalia Ham with pullets roasted
A chine of Beef upon ye side Table
4 dishes of Hot fowle
2 of Pulpitoons
1 Calves head hashed with Livers Larded
A dish of Boiled Salads
A dish of Marrow puddings
A patty of Eels
A Dish of Blanched beans and Bacon Fried
2 Fricasses of Chickens
A Tart de Moij

A dish of veal with sweet bread, roasted and Larded with a Ragout
Pigeons du Poviage
Mackerels Broiled
Whitings buttered with eggs
A Tongue and udder roasted
A Dish of Scotch Collops
A Capon in ye Bladder boiled
A dish of Chardons
Chickens foried
Ducklings foried at la Daube
Eggs in Gravy
Pullets hashed

The Cold Messes

6 Comperts from ye Confectioners
6 of Creames
2 of Pistachios ⎫
2 of Chocolate ⎬ Creames
2 of Ice creame
Potts of Lampries
Collered Eel
Crayfish
Collered Pigg
2 Dishes of Jellyes

2 of Blanc-mange
2 Cold Pigeon Pies
2 of Tarts
2 of Morcills and Truffles
2 of Artichokes
2 of Peas
2 of Champinions
19 Dishes of Porcelain with Small meats interspersed

The Whole 180 dishes of meat all upon ye Table at one time
The Table 5 yards long and 3 yards broade

BILL OF FARE AT WEDDING OF MRS LEVESON'S DAUGHTER TO MR WYNDHAM

A TABLE OF FOWL

Moſt Proper and in Seaſon for the Four Quarters of the Year.

March, April, May.	June, July, Auguſt.	Sept.br, Octo.br, Novem.br	Decem.br, January, Feb.ry
Turkeys with Eggs	Ruffs Reeves Godwits	Wild Ducks	Chickens
Pheasants with Eggs	Knotts Quails Rayls	Teals	Woodcocks
Partridges wth green Corn	Pewets Dottrells	Wild Geese	Snipes
Pullets with Eggs	Pheasant Polts	Barganders	Larks
Green Geese	Young Partridges	Brandgeese	Plovers
Young Ducklins	Heath Polts, Black or	Widgeons	Curlews
Tame Pidgeons	Red Game	Shrilldraks	Redshanks
Squab Pidgeons	Turkey Caponetts	Cackle Ducks	Sea Pheasants
Young Rabbets	Flacking Ducks	Cygnets	Sea Parrots
Young Leverets	Wheat Ears	Pheasants	Shuflers
Caponetts	Virgin Pullets	Partridges	Divers
Chicken Peepers	Young Herons	Grouse	Ox Eyes
Young Turkeys	Young Bitterns	Hares	Pea Cocks & Hens
Tame Ducks	Young Bustards	Rabbets	Bustards
Young Rooks	Pea Polts	Ortelans	Turkeys
Young Sparrows	Wild Pidgeons	Wild Pidgeons	Geese
	Young Coots	Capons	Blackbirds
		Pullets	Feldefares, Thrushes.

USED

MEATS:

THE

PORTER

AT

ASHRIDGE

1652

HE is also to attend diligently at private suppers to receive the meat at the yeomans usher's hands that comes from my table; and place it orderly upon the parlour table for the gentlewomen, that what comes from my table they may make their suppers with.

ASHRIDGE HOUSEHOLD REGULATIONS

... AND THE USHER OF THE HALL AT CANNONS, 1721

That he likewise takes care all the meat that remains not fit for any other use be laid up to be delivered to the poor upon the day or days of the week mentioned in the Instructions.

INSTRUCTIONS TO SERVANTS, CANNONS

... AND AN AMERICAN DUCHESS AT BLENHEIM, 1896

It was the custom at Blenheim to place a basket of tins on the side table in the dining room and here the butler left the remains of our luncheon. It was my duty to cram this food into the tins, which we then carried down to the poorest in the various villages where Marlborough owned property. With a complete lack of fastidiousness it had been the habit to mix meat and vegetables and sweets in a terrible jumble in the same tin. In spite of being considered impertinent for not conforming to precedent, I sorted the various viands into different tins, to the surprise and delight of the recipients.

MEMOIRS OF CONSUELO VANDERBILT

GARLIC, ALLIUM; ... 'tho both by Spaniards and Italians, and the more southern people, familiarly eaten with almost everything ... we absolutely forbid its entrance into our salleting, by reason of its intolerable rankness, and which made it so detested of old that the eating of it was (as we read) part of the punishment for such as had committed the horrid'st crimes. To be sure, 'tis not fit for ladies' palates, nor those who court them, farther than to permit a light touch on the dish with a clove thereof.

Lettuce, LACTUCA SATINA ... ever was, and still continues the principal foundation of the universal tribe of sallets [salads] ... it allays heat, bridles choler, extinguishes thirst, excites appetite, kindly nourishes; and, above all, represses vapours, conciliates sleep, mitigates pain; besides the effect it has on the morals, temperance, and chastity.

Thistle, CARDUUS MARIAE; our Lady's milky or dappled thistle, disarmed of its prickles, and boiled, is worth esteem, and thought to be great breeders of milk, and proper diet for women who are nurses. The young stalk, about May, being peeled and soaked in water, to extract the bitterness, boiled or raw, is a very wholesome sallet, eaten with oil, salt and pepper: some eat them sodden in proper broth or baked in pies, like the artichoke; but the tender stalk boiled or fried, some prefer; both nourishing and restorative.

JOHN EVELYN, *Acetaria: a discourse of sallets* (1699)

(top left) Table of Fowl, from Charles Carter *Complete Cook*, 1730.
(left) Silhouette of an unidentified family at table, c. 1760.

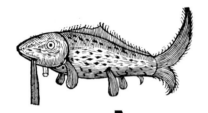

ADDISON IS INSPIRED

1720

ADDISON, according to the tradition of Holland House, used, when composing, to walk up and down the long gallery there, with a bottle of wine at each end of it, which he finished during the operation.

THOMAS MOORE, *Diary*

THE FUNCTIONS OF A DINING-ROOM

1778

THEIR [the French] eating rooms seldom or never constitute a piece in their great apartments, but lie out of the suite, and in fitting them up, little attention is paid to beauty of decoration. The reason of this is obvious; the French meet there only at meals, when they trust to the display of the table for show and magnificence, not to the decoration of the apartment; and as soon as the entertainment is over, they immediately retire to the rooms of the company. It is not so with us. Accustomed by habit, or induced by the nature of our climate, we indulge more largely in the enjoyment of the bottle. Every person of rank here is either a member of the legislation, or entitled by his condition to take part in the political arrangements of his country, and to enter with ardour into those discussions to which they give rise; these circumstances lead men to live more with one another, and more detached from the society of the ladies. The eating rooms are considered as the apartments of conversation, in which we are to pass a great part of our time. This renders it desirable to have them fitted up with elegance and splendour, but in a style different from that of other apartments. Instead of being hung with damask, tapestry, they are always finished with stucco, and ordained with statues and paintings, that they may not retain the smell of the victuals.

ROBERT AND JAMES ADAM, *Works*

CONSPICUOUS CONSUMPTION AT BELVOIR CASTLE

1839

CONSUMPTION of Wine and Ale, Waxlights, &c. from December, 1839, to April, 1840, or about eighteen weeks: Wine, 200 dozen; Ale, 70 Hogsheads; Waxlights, 2330; Sperm-oil, 630 gallons.

Dined at his Grace's table, 1997 persons; in the steward's room, 2421; in the servant's hall, nursery, and kitchen departments, including comers and goers, 11,312 persons.

Of loaves of bread there were consumed 3333; of meat, 22,963 lbs., exclusive of game. The quantity of game killed by his Grace and friends, and consumed at Belvoir Castle alone, was 2589 head.

REV. IRVIN ELLER, *History of Belvoir Castle*

Refreshments in the garden of an unidentified house. Detail from the water-colour by Thomas Robbins, c. 1750.

THERE was no gathering for five o'clock afternoon tea in those days, but most ladies took an hour's rest in their rooms before the six or seven o'clock dinner, retiring thither with their books. Later, young ladies persuaded their maids to bring them surreptitious cups of tea from the housekeeper's room, a practice to which they dared not confess for fear of being well scolded by their elders. Married ladies did not conceal the luxurious habit, as many indulgences were allowed to them which would have been thought highly unnecessary for younger people. It was not till about 1849 or 1850, when I was about twenty-six or twenty-seven that five o'clock tea in the drawing-room was made an institution, and then only in a few fashionable houses where the dinner hour was as late as half-past seven or eight o'clock.

MEMORIES OF GEORGIANA CAROLINE SITWELL

IT was a great treat for us children to be allowed to have tea in the housekeeper's room; where all the choicest cakes, hot toasted buns and every variety of jam were to be found in far greater profusion than in the drawing-room or school-room. There is a story about the great Lord Derby (15th Earl) who complained to his butler about the badness of dinner, and said gravely: 'I do not expect to have as good food as you have in the housekeeper's room, but I must insist on its being the same as in the servant's hall.'

LADY AUGUSTA FANE, *Chit Chat*

ONLY the really improper Edwardians had breakfast in their rooms. The others met, on that Sunday morning, in the dining-room. The smell of last night's port had given place to the smell of this morning's spirits of wine. Rows of little spirit lamps warmed rows of large silver dishes. On a table to the right between the windows were

74

(right) Breakfast in the Carved Room, Petworth House, Sussex. Detail from the water-colour by Mrs Percy Wyndham, c. 1865.

Tea on the terrace before an unidentified country house, c. 1900.

grouped Hams, Tongues, Galantines, Cold Grouse, ditto Pheasant, ditto Partridge, ditto Ptarmigan. No Edwardian meal was complete without Ptarmigan. Hot or Cold. Just Ptarmigan. There would also be a little delicate rectangle of pressed beef from the shop of M. Benoist. On a further table, to the left between the doors, stood fruits of different calibre, and jugs of cold water, and jugs of lemonade. A fourth table contained porridge utensils. A fifth coffee, and pots of Indian and China tea. The latter were differentiated from each other by little ribbons of yellow (indicating China) and of red (indicating, without *arrière pensée*, our Indian Empire). The centre table, which was prepared for twenty-three people, would be bright with Malmaisons and toast-racks. No newspapers were, at that stage, allowed.

The atmosphere of the Edwardian dining-room at nine-thirty was essentially daring. A pleasant sense of confederacy and sin hung above the smell of the spirit-lamps. For had they not all been brought up to attend family prayers? And had they not all eluded that obligation? It was true, of course, that the host and hostess, with their niece, had at nine proceeded to the family chapel and heard the butler reading a collect for the day. But the guests had for their part evaded these Victorian obligations. This corporate evasion gave to the proceedings an atmosphere of dash. There was no insincerity in the bright gaiety with which they greeted each other, with which they discussed how he or she had slept. 'A little kedjiree, Lady Maude?' 'Oh, thank you, Mr Stapleton.' Evidently it was all going very well.

Edwardian breakfasts were in no sense a hurried proceeding. The porridge was disposed of negligently, people walking about and watching the rain descend upon the Italian garden. Then would come whiting and omelette and devilled kidneys and little fishy messes in shells. And then tongue and ham and a slice of Ptarmigan. And then scones and honey and marmalade. And then a little melon, and a nectarine or two, and just one or two of those delicious raspberries. The men at that stage would drift (I employ the accepted term) to the smoking-room. The women would idle in the saloon watching the rain descend upon the Italian garden. It was then 10.30.

HAROLD NICOLSON, *Small Talk*

ONE custom particularly delighted us at Bowood. It was a sort of survival of the former *fêtes champêtres*. Lady Lansdowne ('Granny Maud', as she was called by her grandchildren) would ask the guests after break-fast whether they would like a picnic lunch as a change if 'Daddy Clan' (Lord Lansdowne) thought it would be fine enough. On his approval being given, the arrangements were made. On the first occasion I assumed that this would entail a walk or drive, by car or carriage, and perhaps an uncomfortable but agreeable lunch in a wood or on the side of a hill. As the hours . . . passed I began to wonder what was going to happen. At one o'clock we were ready to start, and the little company walked about two or three hundred yards from the house to the lake. At the lakeside was a boat-house, and a kind of chalet or summer-house . . . The luncheon had been carried down; the tables were arranged in the same silver and glass and napery as would have been used in the house. The butler and one or two footmen were there to serve. In fact the picnic was no different from an ordinary lunch, except that we ventured a few hundred yards from the mansion, and sat above the boat house. After luncheon and all the suitable wines had been served and coffee drunk, we processed back to the house. The great expedition had taken place.

HAROLD MACMILLAN, *Winds of Change*

Breakfast at Sunningdale Park, Berkshire, photographed by Alexandra, Princess of Wales, c. 1889.
(right) The Duke of Clarence and Princess Mary of Teck, photographed in the conservatory of Luton Hoo, Bedfordshire, after their engagement in December 1891.

5
Love,
Lust
&
Marriage

*U*p till the eighteenth century almost all country-house marriages were arranged. From then on, if not arranged they were at least engineered. Daughters were introduced to the right young men, and vice versa. Lady Stanley of Alderley could afford to write indulgently about her daughter's courtship in the 1860s. It was an earl who was courting her.

Many arranged marriages turned out happily. Conscientious parents would not push their children into marrying someone with whom they were obviously imcompatible. However, country-house life allowed couples who had merged on the basis of property and good connections, rather than love or even respect, to go their own way after marriage – within reason. They could move into different parts of the same house, or into different houses. Husbands could keep mistresses, as long as they were not kept in the same house as their wives. It was acceptable, and even usual, for a mistress to be of a lower social class, but unacceptable, in this case, for her lover to marry her. Lady Harington's isolation was largely due to the fact that she had been both an actress and her husband's mistress before marriage. County society would never have visited her at Elvaston Castle, had it been invited.

Upper-class wives could take lovers, as long as they were reasonably discreet about it – and had produced a *bona-fide* heir first. Wilfred Scawen Blunt was keeping the conventions by creeping secretly across the moonlit hall at Parham – but breaking them because he was heading for a newly-married wife. Lady Caroline Lamb broke all the conventions because she made her feelings about Byron public – even doing such silly things as slashing her wrists in front of him at a London ball. She was frozen out of London as a result.

There were plenty of exceptions to the general pattern. There were love-matches and elopements, from the earliest years. There were couples who stayed devoted to each other all their lives. And there were county girls who went completely to the bad, like Bess Broughton, who ran off from a Herefordshire manor house in the seventeenth century, and became one of the most notorious of London prostitutes.

OLAVE SHARINGTON WINS A HUSBAND AT LACOCK ABBEY

DAME Olave, a daughter and co-heir of Sir Henry Sharington, of Lacock, being in love with John Talbot, a younger brother of the Earl of Shrewsbury, and her father not consenting that she should marry him; discoursing with him one night from the battlements, said she, I will leap down to you. Her sweetheart replied, he would catch her then; but he did not believe she would have done it. She leapt down, and the wind, which was then high, came under her coats and did something break the fall. Mr Talbot caught her in his arms, but she struck him dead: she cried out for help, and he was with great difficulty brought to life again. Her father told her that since she had made such a leap she should e'en marry him. She was my honoured friend Col. Sharington Talbot's grandmother, and died at her house at Lacock about 1651, being about an hundred years old.

JOHN AUBREY, *Brief Lives*

THE COUNTESS OF PEMBROKE AT WILTON C. 1580

SHE was a beautiful lady and had an excellent wit, and had the best breeding that that age could afford. She had a pretty sharp-oval face. Her hair was of reddish yellow.

She was very salacious, and she had a contrivance that in the spring of the year when the stallions were to leap the mares they were to be brought before such a part of the house, where she had a *vidette* to look on them and please herself with their sport; and then she would act the like sport herself with *her* stallions. One of her great gallants was crook-back't Cecil, earl of Salisbury.

JOHN AUBREY, *Brief Lives*

(left) Madame Baccelli, mistress of the 3rd Duke of Dorset, being painted by Gainsborough in the ballroom at Knole. From a drawing of c. 1782, possibly by Ozias Humphrey.

A young man serenading a lady before Aylesford Friary, Kent. Detail from a painting of c.1650 by an unidentified artist.

MISTRESS Elizabeth Broughton was daughter of Broughton in Herefordshire, an ancient family. Her father lived at the manor-house at Canon-Peon. Whether she was born there or no, I know not: but there she lost her maiden-head to a poor young fellow, then I believe handsome, but, in 1660, a pitiful poor old weaver, clerk of the parish. He had fine curled hair, but grey. Her father at length discovered her inclinations and locked her up in the turret of the house, but she gets down by a rope; and away she got to London, and did set-up for her self.

She was a most exquisite beauty, as finely shaped as nature could frame; and had a delicate wit. She was soon taken notice of at London, and her price was very dear.

JOHN AUBREY, *Brief Lives*

A match had been arranged between Philip Carteret and Lady Jemima Montagu, daughter of Pepys's patron and former employer, the Earl of Sandwich. In July 1665 Pepys took the young man to meet his future wife at Dagnans, in Essex.

JULY 15, 1665 . . . but Lord, what silly discourse we had by the way as to matter of love-making, he being the most awkward man ever I met withal in my life as to that business. Thither we came by time it begin to be dark, and were kindly received by my Lady Wright and my Lord Crew; and to discourse they went, my Lord discoursing with him, asking him questions of travel, which he answered well enough in a few words. But nothing to the lady from him at all. To supper, and after supper to talk again, he yet taking no notice of the lady. My Lord would have had me have consented to leaving the young people together tonight to begin their amours, his staying being but to be little. But I advised against it, lest the lady might be too much surprised. So they led him up to his chamber, where I stayed a little to know how he liked the lady; which he told me he did mightily, but Lord, in the dullest insipid manner

that ever lover did. So I bid him good-night, and down to prayers with my Lord Crew's family . . .

July 16. LORD'S DAY . . . Having trimmed myself, down to Mr Carteret; and he being ready, we down and walked in the gallery an hour to two . . . Here I taught him what to do; to take the lady always by the hand to lead her; and telling him that I would find opportunity to leave them two together, he should make these and these compliments, and also take time to do the like to my Lord Crew and Lady Wright. After I had instructed him, which he thanked me for, owning that he needed my teaching him, my Lord Crew came down and family, the young lady among the rest; and so by coaches to church . . .

Thence back again by coach – Mr Carteret having not had the confidence to take this lady once by the hand, coming or going; which I told him of when we came home, and he will hereafter do it. So to dinner . . . Then to walk in the gallery and to sit down. By and by my Lady Wright and I go out (and then my Lord Crew, he not by design); and lastly my Lady Crew came out and

left the young people together. And a little pretty daughter of my Lady Wright's most innocently came out afterward, and shut the door to, as if she had done it, poor child, by inspiration – which made me without have good sport to laugh at.

They together an hour; and by and by church time, whither he led her into the coach . . . So home again and to walk in the gardens, where we left the young couple a second time . . .

July 17. Up, all of us, and to billiards . . . By and by the young couple left together. Anon to dinner . . . Before we went, I took my Lady Jem apart and would know how she liked this gentleman and whether she was under any difficulty concerning him. She blushed and hid her face awhile, but at last I forced her to tell me; she answered that she could readily obey what her father and mother had done – which was all she could say or I expect . . .

July 24 . . . I find Mr Carteret yet as backward almost in his caresses as he was the first day.

The wedding took place on July 31. Pepys set out for it 'being in my new coloured-silk suit and coat, trimmed with gold buttons and gold broad lace

83

A bedroom in the Nostell Priory doll's house, c. 1740.

round my hands, very rich and fine.' *Owing to a muddle over the coach, he missed the service. However:-* ... so to dinner, and very merry we were ... At night to supper, and so to talk and, which methought was the most extraordinary thing, all of us to prayers as usual, and the young bride and bridegroom too. And so after prayers, soberly to bed; only, I got into the bridegroom's chamber while he undressed himself, and there was very merry – till he was called to the bride's chamber and into bed they went. I kissed the bride in bed, and so the curtains drawn with the greatest gravity that could be, and so goodnight.

SAMUEL PEPYS, *Diary*

84

A young girl dreams of balls and Byron at her dressing table. From the drawing by Olivia de Ros, c. 1820.

LADY CAROLINE LAMB HOLDS AN AUTO-DA-FÉ AT BROCKET HALL 1812

BYRON at last was sick of her. When their intimacy was at an end, and while she was living in the country, she burned, very solemnly, on a sort of funeral pile, *transcripts* of all the letters which she had received from Byron, and a *copy* of a miniature (his portrait) which he had presented to her; several girls from the neighbourhood, whom she had dressed in white garments, dancing round the pile, and singing a song which she had written for the occasion.

SAMUEL ROGERS, *Table Talk*

Lady Caroline recited the following verses by the bonfire, dressed in her favourite costume as a page.

See here are locks and braids of coloured hair
Worn oft by me, to make the people stare;
Rouge, feathers, flowers, and all those tawdry things,
Besides those Pictures, letters, chains, and rings –
All made to lure the mind and please the eye,
And fill the heart with pride and vanity –
Burn, fire, burn; these glittering toys destroy.
While thus we hail the blaze with throats of joy.
Burn, fire, burn, while wondering Boys exclaim,
And gold and trinkets glitter in the flame.
Ah! look not thus on me, so grave, so sad;
Shake not your heads, nor say the Lady's mad.
Judge not of others, for there is but one
To whom the heart and feelings can be known.
Upon my youthful faults few censures cast.
Look to the future – and forgive the past.
London, farewell; vain world, vain life, adieu!
Take the last tears I e'er shall shed for you.
Young tho' I seem, I leave the world for ever,
Never to enter it again – no, never – never!

LORD

AND

LADY

HARRING-

TON

AT

HOME

1835

ANOTHER castle with which I was very familiar was Elvaston, near Derby, where year after year I stayed with the late Lord and Lady Harrington. Originally a red-brick manor house, it was castellated in the days of Wyatt; and though architects of today would smile at its artificial Gothic, it may now for this very reason be regarded as an historical monument. It is a monument of tastes and sentiments which have long since passed away. It represents not only a vanished taste in architecture, but sentiments also which are now even more remote. The Earl of Harrington, under whom the Gothic transfiguration was accomplished, seems to have regarded himself as a species of knight-errant. Round the fluted pillars by which the roof of the hall is supported – a hall which he christened 'the hall of the fair star' – were strapped imitation lances, and the windows were darkened by scrolls which all bore the same motto, 'Loyal to Honour and to Beauty'. This Lord Harrington had married a very beautiful wife, for whose pleasure he surrounded the house with a labyrinth of clipped yew hedges, the trees having been brought full grown from every part of England. Animated by a romantic jealousy, he never permitted this lady to stray beyond the park gates, and a little pavilion at the end of a yew avenue contains, or contained till lately, a curious something which is a vivid revelation of his mind. It consists of an image in plaster-of-Paris of his lady-love, together with one of himself kneeling at her feet and gazing at her, his hands being about to commit his adoration to the strings of a guitar.

W. H. MALLOCK, *Memoirs of Life and Literature*

Love on a bicycle. Detail of a frieze at Paddockhurst House, Sussex, designed by Walter Crane, c.1897.

BARBARA
TASBURGH
ELOPES
FROM
BURGH-
WALLIS
HALL
1839

I was greatl‹
grieved to leav‹
my poor, long
suffering mother
who had been s‹
unvariedly kin‹
to me. I hardl‹
know how I kep‹
from breakin›
down. She alway‹
went to be‹
early, and afte‹
kissing her a‹
usual on partin›
for the night I retired to my ow‹
room, locked myself in, an‹
changed my light-coloure‹
summer frock for one of a darł
cachemire.

As for the watch-dog that wa‹
kennelled under my bedroon‹
window to keep guard over m‹
slumbers, the good Mrs Firtł
gave it some harmless dru›
which removed the danger fron‹
that direction. At half-pas‹
eleven I lit up my room, opene‹
wide the window, and sat dow‹
to wait. At a quarter to mid
night, on Wednesday the 19tł
June, William was under m‹
window, having posted fron‹
Doncaster and left the chaise a‹
the end of the lane so that th‹
noise of wheels should not dis‹
turb the house. I threw my sof‹
bundle of belongings out of th‹
window, and then by means o‹
torn-up sheets fastened to ‹
heavy, old-fashioned sofa, ‹
swung out and, wonderful t‹
say, got down without a scratch
We ran for our lives to where th‹
chaise was standing, the object o‹
getting posters from Doncaste‹
instead of from Robin Hood'‹
Well (only a mile from Burgh
wallis) being to leave no clu‹
behind for pursuit in th‹
morning.

We posted through the night

and all next day, until we reached the Blacksmith's house at Gretna Green at 6 p.m. on the evening of June 20th, when we became man and wife.

L.E.O. CHARLTON, *Recollections of a Northumbrian Lady*

(left) The Marquess and Marchioness of Lansdowne at a window of Bowood House, Wiltshire, in 1870, shortly after their marriage.
(above) A young man plays his flute for the ladies at Dynes Hall. Diana Sperling, *c.*1815–20.

THE

EARL

OF

AIRLIE

PROPOSES

AT

ALDERLEY

HALL

1851

AUGUST 3.

He never leaves her side for a moment, & she seems very well pleased, & they are now, between 12 & 1, sitting on the lawn with a book each, but I can see by the reflection in the window that he is not reading. I do not know why he does not settle it, Blanche says she gives him every opportunity, but her manner is rather brusque and perhaps he is a little afraid, & she every now & then says very odd things. But all is in a right train & I hardly think she would make such a slave of him if she did not mean to reward him.

August 4.

It is all settled, & I do hope it will be for our darling's happiness – I never saw more deep feeling than on his part, & tho' Blanche is very nervous yet she is glad it is settled. During their ride he asked her if she would care for a dog, if he gave her one, & when she came home she went upstairs to rest. I saw at dinner he was very nervous & that he was most anxious to speak. I had given her a red carnation (like those I used to give you) to give him, at first she said she would not, but she came down with the heath in her hair he had got for her & waited on the stair case to give him the flower – he never spoke but looked very pale. After dinner he rushed after her, & she went with him to sit on two chairs under the brown beech, & then we all walked out, they turned up the Fernhill & we walked all about the boy's walk. When we came home I saw him alone & he came & took my arm & walked me away in the dark, & he could not speak so I was obliged to begin, & then he told me he had spoken to her & that 'she had no great objection', that he loved her very much – had done so for two years – that he had been very unhappy the last week because he thought she never would like him. I said then why *would* you go to Goodwood – he said he was obliged to do so. After some talk I left him to go to Blanche, & found her on her knees in her room, very nervous, but much happier, & then she told me how it all happened, that they went off walking & he never spoke all the time till she grew so faint & cold she said she must sit down. He then said he hoped she would not be angry but he must speak – she covered her face with her hands & he went on & said he was neither as good nor as clever as she was, but that he loved her very much, & she never answering till she says he took her hand & spoke in such agony & told her she frightened him, & then she answered that she would try to make him happy, but she said her voice sounded cold & different to his. She then asked him if he cld. give up the thing he liked best for her, meaning racing, & he said he would, & she asked him if he had ever loved Lady Rachel at which he laughed & said never. She also asked him if he had ever liked anyone & he said he had been in love with Martia Fox, & she was kind enough to say that she did not mind that as she was dead, & was very good – & after such talk she went upstairs.

LADY STANLEY OF ALDERLEY TO LORD STANLEY

'Doll' is Lady Zouche, recently and unhappily married. She ran off from her husband shortly after this incident – but not with Blunt. His account is a mixture of reminiscence, and diary entries made at the time.

A

SUSSEX

AFFAIR:

WILFRED

SCAWEN

BLUNT

FALLS

FOR

HIS

HOSTESS

AT

PARHAM

1875

THE week that followed

was a week of extravagant amusement, one of sublime unreason in an Earthly Paradise, for Parham is in all Sussex, and therefore in all England, the perfectest and best, the most ideal framework of romance. Its old park and its ancient trees, its oaks and thorns and knee deep fern, set at the foot of the downs, from which ten minutes takes a rider to the top where he will meet the breezes from the sea, the wide heaths stretching northwards, the great fir wood where the herons breed, and the Tudor glories of the house, all these beautiful and noble things were then combined, to make a play ground for us during just that week, a week of riotous profanity which grieves my conscience yet, and was then to be shut up for us and lost for ever ... I was ensorcelled with Doll's gipsy face, with her sudden love for me and the romance of

Gentlemen of the Bootle-Wilbraham family paying homage before Lathom House, Lancashire, 1904.

the situation. To have foregone playing the leading part in such a drama when thus thrust upon me was an impossibility of what was in my nature. During that enchanted week I saw her as the sleeping beauty to be called to life by her prince of fairyland and I resolved it should be my hand to wake her. If it was not mine it would be another's, this was clear. Robin had lost all control over the situation; he seemed already to have abdicated his marital right, and she was too pretty to be long without a lover . . .

The week went by in imitation of the wild life we were supposed to be about to lead in Abyssinia. The weather was perfect for the purpose and we were to live as far as possible out of doors. Doll was in her nature a gipsy and this was entirely to her mind.

September 13 . . . Suddenly it was resolved we should sleep tonight in the North Park Woods and we fixed on the heronry as our place of encampment. Beds were robbed of their blankets, the kitchen of its cooking pots, a cart was ordered to the door and loaded with the spoils . . . We made our fire under the giant fir trees, ranging our sleeping places round it, while Pompey roasted partridges upon a wooden spit. One huge bed was spread for all the party which we called the 'Bed of Ware', and we sat talking far into the night. Doll in her ulster coat a true gipsy, had hung a piece of looking glass near her on a tree and was tired now after her long day of violent life, and sad and tender. She sat watching me with great black eyes in the firelight . . . At last we lay down, our pillows almost touching and our faces. It was long before we slept. The fire burned at first too brightly and the moon was nearly at its full. After the rest were silent we two were still awake and always when I looked at her her eyes were wide and fixed on mine. There were rooks above us which fidgeted overhead, and once a heron coming back to roost settled a moment, then with a ghostly croak seeing there were strangers there flapped hurriedly away ... At last the fire burned down and the moon set ... That was our marriage night ...

The days and nights that followed were hardly less an enchantment. Parham was a ghostly house in which to wander by moonlight and every night I passed from the East Wing where my room was placed to hers in the West Wing, descending a stair and then ascending, and passing between the two stairs through the uncurtained hall watched by the moon and by the effigies in armour. In this lay the romance close bound up with the risk, the dangers of discovery. She, reckless child, feared nothing. All she asked was to be free of the last tie that bound her to her legal lord. He had been useless to her as a husband, and she held him cheap. When at our last night's end Sept. 19, it was time for us to go home, Doll tearful at parting made me take with me her wedding ring. I am to give her another in its place. We are to love each other for ten years, since it is best to fix a limit to all human happiness, and we are to meet again in London on Tuesday, and on the 30th for another week at Crabbet.

BLUNT MSS, FITZWILLIAM MUSEUM

AN

UNFORTU-

NATE

MISTAKE

C. 1880

EVEN the craftiest did not always succeed in his strategems. Lord Charles Beresford told my grandfather that on one occasion he tiptoed into a dark room and jumped into the vast bed shouting 'Cock-a-doodle-doo', to find himself, when trembling hands had lit a paraffin lamp, between the Bishop of Chester and his wife. The situation seemed very difficult to explain and he left the house before breakfast next morning.

ANITA LESLIE, *Edwardians in Love*

(right) Lord Nelson and Emma Hamilton entering the grounds of Fonthill Abbey, Wiltshire, 1801.

6
Parties

*P*arties in country houses originated to cele-
brate particular events: feasts, especially
Christmas and the New Year; births, marriages,
and funerals; and the paying of rent by tenants.
They invariably involved eating and drinking, and
were sometimes followed by dancing. A party was
no good unless it involved gorging and getting
drunk.

Over the centuries the range and types of parties were extended. House-warming parties, servants' balls and coming-of-age parties all appeared in the eighteenth century, and perhaps a little before. Garden parties were a nineteenth-century development. They were a response to increasing numbers of middle-class families living in country neighbourhoods, who were too grand to be invited to tenant's balls and not grand enough to be asked to dinner. Hence the abbreviation GPO, for 'Garden Party Only' which Mrs Sothill in Evelyn Waugh's *Put Out More Flags* affixed to certain names in her address book.

In earlier days there was a distinction between parties in country houses, which were attended by all classes, and parties in London, which were aimed at the fashionable. Funerals took place in the country, christening and parties to launch daughters were more often held in London. The right kinds of godparents and young men could more easily be gathered together there.

As transport improved, and the lesser gentry learned social graces in provincial assembly rooms, London-type parties began to be introduced to the country. The eighteenth-century type of ball was a London invention: the emphasis was on dancing rather than eating or drinking, and only upper-class guests were invited. Towards the end of the century, balls began to be given in country houses; but the reaction of guests to the ball at Fawley Court, in 1777, is still 'Sure, we are in London'.

The belief that landowners had a duty to entertain their tenantry, especially at Christmas, dates back to the Middle Ages. In the early seventeenth century James I attacked country-house owners for getting too fond of London life. He issued a series of edicts, ordering them to return to their houses for Christmas, and entertain their tenantry in the traditional manner. There is, in fact, a long history behind the parties for tenants or the village described with such different inflections by Dorothy Henley and Cecil Beaton.

The Hellfire-Club fancy-dress party at West Wycombe Park, Buckinghamshire, June, 1953. Sir John and Lady Dashwood with the Marchioness of Dufferin and Ava, Roy and Billa Harrod and other friends.

The setting is probably Apthorpe, in Northamptonshire

HARVEST-

HOME

AT

THE

EARL

OF

WESTMOR-

LAND'S

Come, Sons of Summer, by whose toil,
We are the Lords of Wine and Oil:
By whose tough labours, and rough hands,
We rip up first, then reap our lands.
Crown'd with the ears of corn, now come,
And, to the Pipe, sing Harvest home.
Come forth, my Lord, and see the Cart
Dressed up with all the Country Art.
See, here a *Maukin*, there a sheet,
As spotless pure, as it is sweet:
The Horses, Mares, and frisking Fillies,
(Clad, all, in Linen, white as Lilies.)
The Harvest Swains, and Wenches bound
For joy, to see the *Hock-cart* crown'd.
About the Cart, hear, how the Rout
Of Rural Younglings raise the shout;
Pressing before, some coming after,
Those with a shout, and these with laughter.
Some bless the Cart; some kiss the sheaves;
Some prank them up with Oaken leaves:
Some cross the Fill-horse: some with great
Devotion, stroke the home-borne wheat:
While other Rusticks, less attent
To Prayers, than to Merryment,
Run after with their breeches rent.
Well, on, brave boys, to your Lord's Hearth,
Glitt'ring with fire; where, for your mirth,
Ye shall see first the large and chief
Foundation of your Feast, Fat Beef:
With Upper Stories, Mutton, Veal
And Bacon, (which makes full the meal)
With sev'rall dishes standing by,
As here a Custard, there a Pie,
And here all-tempting Frumentie.
And for to make the merry cheer,
If smirking Wine be wanting here,
There's that, which drowns all care, stout Beer:
Which freely drink to your Lords health,
Then to the Plough, (the Common-wealth)
Next to your Flails, your Fanes, your Fats;
Then to the Maids with Wheaten-Hats:
To the rough Sickle, and crook Scythe,
Drink, frolic, boys, till all be blyth.

From ROBERT HERRICK, *The Hock-cart or Harvest Home*

I dined at Stowe yesterday, Nelly Denton and Jock Stewkeley went with me. We met Sir Harry Andrews, & his lady and daughter, his only child there, as also cousin Risley & his lady & Jack Doddington, & 3 sisters of Lady Temple, & Mr Stanion, husband to one of them, & Ned Andrews and Groves his father-in-law, & Thomas Temple & another old Temple with 3 or 4 very drunken parsons, which made up our company. Lady Baltinglass was invited & promised to be there but failed. We saw Sir Richard and his fine lady wedded, & flung the stocking, & then left them to themselves, & so in this manner was ended the celebration of his Marriage à la mode. After that we had Music, Feasting, Drinking, Revelling, Dancing & Kissing: it was two of the clock this morning before we got home.

EDMUND VERNEY TO SIR ROBERT VERNEY, 26 AUGUST, 1675

On Thursday last Jacob Houblon, of Hallingbury in Essex, Esq., member of Parliament for Colchester, baptized his new born son with the greatest magnificence imaginable. Most of the gentlemen within 15 or 20 miles of Mr Houblon's seat in Essex were present, and most of the common people within 4 or 5 miles were made so welcome that they lay in heaps round his house dead drunk. There were three courses of upwards of 200 dishes each, and two tables, at which were 400 persons serv'd all at once, with all sorts of rarities and sweetmeats. Sir John Hynd Cotton and Sir Robert Abdy, Barts, were godfathers, the latter being proxy for Dr Houblon, and the child was nam'd Jacob. There was a grand concert of music at dinner, and a noble ball at night, from which the company did not break up till the next morning. There were 20 Knights and Baronets, and 150 gentlemen, and about as many ladies.

Daily Gazetteer, 14 SEPTEMBER, 1736

Col. Pl. VIII (right) Preparations for a tenant's dinner in the Great Hall, Cotehele, Cornwall. Lithograph after Nicholas Condy, c.1840.

SIR

WATKIN

WILLIAMS

WYNN

COMES

OF

AGE

AT

WYNNSTAY

1770

AT noon, not less than twenty thousand visitants were assembled ... among the hecatombs sacrified to his friends, an enormous ox was roasted whole, which being placed upon a kind of triumphant car, ornamented with garlands and streamers, was drawn, by six little mountaineers, to the amphitheatre in the midst of which was erected a Bacchanalian altar, crowned with a cask, the size of which presented a suitable emblem of that unbounded hospitality so long renowned at Wynnstay ... When Sir Watkin, from an eminence, gave his guests a general salute in a bumper, their repeated acclamations, mixed with the thunder of cannon, might fairly be said to make the adjacent Welsh mountains tremble. While the populace here regaled, the numerous visitants of superior rank were summoned, by sound of trumpet, to dinner ...

DIARY OF ELIZABETH, DUCHESS OF NORTHUMBERLAND

Sir Watkin Williams Wynn's private theatre at Wynnstay, Denbighshire, from an engraved ticket of 1782.
Col. Pl. IX (left) An assembly at Wanstead House, Essex, 1729. Detail from the painting by William Hogarth.

MRS

PHILIP

LYBBE

POWYS

GOES

TO

SUPPER

AT

FAWLEY

PARK

1777

O N the Wednesday, Mr. and Miss Pratt, my brother, and ourselves got to Freemans' a little after eight. So great a crowd, or so fine a house to dispose them in, you don't often see in the country . . . Their usual eating-room not being large enough, the supper was in the hall, so that we did not come in thro' that, but a window was taken out of the library, and a temporary flight of steps made into that, from which we passed into the green breakfast-room (that night the tea-room), thro' the pink paper billiard-room, along the saloon, into the red damask drawing-room. Though none sat down, this room was soon so crowded as to make us return to the saloon. This likewise very soon fill'd, and as the tea was carrying round, one heard from every one, 'Fine assembly,' 'Magnificent house,' 'Sure we are in London.'

They danc'd in the saloon. No minuets that night; would have been difficult without a master of the ceremonies among so many people of rank. Two card-rooms, the drawing-room and eating-room. The latter looked so elegant lighted up; two tables at loo, one quinze, one vingt-une, many whist. At one of the former large sums pass'd and repass'd. I saw one lady of quality borrow ten pieces of Tessier within half-an-hour after she set down to vingt-une, and a countess at loo who ow'd to every soul round the table before half the night was over. They wanted Powys and I to play at 'low loo,' as they term'd it, but we rather chose to keep our features less agitated than those we saw around us, for I always observe even those who have it to lose have no less a tinge of the rouge in their countenances when fortune does not smile. Oh! what a disfiguring thing is gaming, particularly to the ladies.

The orgeat, lemonade, capillaire, and red and white negus, with cakes, were carried round the whole evening. At half an hour after twelve the supper was announced, and the hall doors thrown open, on entering which nothing could be more striking, as you know 'tis so fine a one, and was then illuminated by three hundred colour'd lamps round the six doors, over the chimney, and over the statue at the other end. The tables were a long one down the room, terminated by a crescent at each end, and a crescent table against the two doors in the middle; the windows were sideboards. The tables had a most pleasing effect, ornamented with everything in the confectionery way, and festoons and wreaths of artificial flowers prettily disposed; all fruits of the season, as grapes, pines, &c.; fine wines (Freeman is always famous for); everything conducted with great ease – no bustle. Their servants are particularly clever on these occasions, indeed are annually used to it, and none of those of the company admitted, which generally creates confusion.

Ninety-two sat down to supper. Everybody seem'd surpris'd at entering the hall. The house had before been amazingly admir'd, but now there was one general exclamation of wonder. This, you may be certain, pleas'd the owners, particularly as many of the nobility there now never saw it before. The once so beautiful Lady Almeria, I think, is vastly altered. She and Lady Harriot Herbert had the new trimmings, very like bell-ropes with their tassels, and seemingly very inconvenient in dancing. Lady Villiers had a very pretty ornament on, which was the girdle 'Lady Townly' wore, fasten'd round the robing of her gown, and hung down as a tippet. After supper they return'd to dancing, chiefly then cotillons, till near six.

CAROLINE POWYS *Letters*, 13 JANUARY, 1777

Mr Richard Edgcumbe entertaining his guests before the Garden House at Mount Edgcumbe, Cornwall. Thomas Badeslade, 1735.

MAGIC

AT

STOWE:

PRINCESS

AMELIA

ENTERTAINED

1764

ALL day a number of people were preparing the grotto and garden for Her Highness and company to sup there ... At ten the gardens were illuminated with above a thousand lights, and the water before the grotto was covered with floating lights. At the farther end of the canal on the ship, which was curiously figured with lights, was a place for the music, which performed all supper-time ... Her Highness walked down to the grotto at half-past ten, and was pleased and delighted with the grand prospect which was presented to her view; nothing was seen but lights and people, nothing was heard but music and fireworks, and nothing was felt but joy and happiness.

GRENVILLE PAPERS

Peasants dancing under the portico of Stowe House, Buckinghamshire, at the coming-of-age of Earl Temple, February, 1818.

On Wednesday a small Vauxhall was acted for us at the grotto in the Elysian fields, which was illuminated with lamps as were the thicket and two little barks on the lake. The evening was more than cool, and the destined spot anything but dry. There were not half lamps enough, and no music but an ancient militia man who played cruelly on the squeaking tabor and pipe. As our procession descended the vast flight of steps into the garden, in which was assembled a crowd of people from Buckingham and the neighbouring villages, I could not help laughing as I surveyed our troop, which, instead of tripping lightly to such an Arcadian entertainment were hobbling down by the balustrades, wrapped in cloaks and great coats, for fear of catching cold . . . We were none of us young enough for a pastoral.

HORACE WALPOLE TO GEORGE MONTAGU, 7 JULY, 1770

LORD

NELSON

AND

EMMA

VISIT

FONTHILL

ABBEY

1801

THEY all proceeded slowly and in order, as the dark of the evening was growing into darkness. In about three quarters of an hour, soon after having entered the great wall which includes the abbey-woods, the procession passed a noble Gothic arch . . . and hence, upon a road winding through the woods of pine and fir, brightly illuminated by innumerable lamps hung in the trees, and by flambeaux moving with the carriages, they proceeded betwixt two divisions of the Fonthill volunteers, accompanied by their band playing solemn marches, the effect of which was much heightened by the continued roll of drums placed at different distances on the hills . . .

The company on their arrival at the Abbey could not fail to be struck with the increasing splendour of lights and their effects, contrasted with the deep shades which fell on the walls, battlements, and turrets, of the different groups of the edifice. Some parts of the light struck on the walls and arches of

the great tower, till it vanished by degrees into an awful gloom at its summit . . .

The parties, alighting in orderly succession from their carriages, entered a groined Gothic hall through a double line of soldiers. From thence they were received into the great saloon, called the Cardinal's parlour, furnished with rich tapestries, long curtains of purple damask before the arched windows, ebony tables and chairs studded with ivory, of various but antique fashion; the whole room in the noblest style of monastic ornament, and illuminated by lights on silver sconces. At the moment of entrance they sat down at a long table, occupying nearly the whole length of the room (53 feet), to a superb dinner, served in one long line of enormous silver dishes, in the substantial *costume* of the ancient abbeys, unmixed with the refinements of modern cookery. The table and side-boards glittering with piles of plate and a profusion of candle-lights, not to mention a blazing Christmas fire of cedar and the cones of pine, united to increase the splendour and to improve the *coup'-d'oeil* of the room . . .

Dinner being ended, the company removed up stairs to the other finished apartments of the abbey. The staircase was lighted by certain mysterious living figures at different intervals, dressed in hooded gowns, and standing with large wax-torches in their hands. A magnificent room hung with yellow damask, and decorated with cabinets of the most precious japan, received the assembly. It was impossible not to be struck, among other objects, with its credences, (or antique buffets) exhibiting much treasure of wrought plate, cups, vases, and ewers of solid gold. It was from this room they passed into the Library, fitted up with the same appropriate taste. The Library opens by a large Gothic screen into the gallery . . . This room, which when finished will be more than 270 feet long, is to half that length completely fitted up, and furnished in the most impressively monastic style. A superb shrine, with a beautiful statue of St. Anthony in marble and alabaster, the work of Rossi, placed upon it, with reliquaries studded with brilliants of immense value, the whole illuminated by a grand display of wax-lights on candle-sticks and candelabras of massive silver gilt, exhibited a scene at once strikingly splendid and awfully magnificent . . .

As the company entered the gallery a solemn music struck the ear from some invisible quarter, as if from behind the screen of scarlet curtains which backed the shrine, or from its canopy above, and suggested ideas of a religious service; ... After the scenic representation a collation was presented in the library, consisting of various sorts of confectionery served in gold baskets, with spiced wines, &c. whilst rows of chairs were placed in the great room beyond, which had first received the company above stairs. A large vacant space was left in the front of the seats. The assembly no sooner occupied them than Lady Hamilton appeared in the character of Agrippina, bearing the ashes of Germanicus in a golden urn, and as presenting herself before the Roman people with the design of exciting them to revenge the death of her husband ... Lady Hamilton displayed, with truth and energy, every gesture, attitude, and expression of countenance, which could be conceived as Agrippina herself, best calculated to have moved the passions of the Romans in behalf of their favourite general. The action of her head, of her hands and arms in the various positions of it, in her manner of presenting before the Romans, or of holding it up to the gods in the act of supplication was most classically graceful ... The company delighted and charmed broke up, and departed at 11 o'clock ... On leaving this strange nocturnal scene of vast buildings and extensive forest, now rendered dimly and partially visible by the declining light of lamps and torches, and the twinkling of a few scattered stars in a clouded sky, the company seemed, as soon as they had passed the sacred boundary of the great wall, as if waking from a dream, or just freed from the influence of some magic spell ...

Gentleman's Magazine, APRIL, 1801

Tenants and labourers being feasted in front of Stowe, February 1818.

THE cricket matches were the highlights of the summer holidays, one eleven staying in the house, and a neighbouring house bringing over the other ... The first steps of making friends with strangers took longer than nowadays; we did not plunge into Christian names and familiarity all at once, by any means, and dinner on the first night when the cricket eleven had collected was often stiff and rather painful; everybody sat looking straight in front of them, or at their plates, while laborious conversation was conscientiously made. On the first evening no one was ever found who could sing, or play, or do any tricks, but all this ice melted after one day's cricket, and by the second evening all kinds of latent powers were discovered in the guests, prodigies who could bend backwards, or could pick up an orange with their teeth from the floor, or play entrancingly on their combs. All through the day in the sun, or, worse, in a chill wind, we sat riveted by the game, going through agonies of despair and sympathy with the unsuccessful players. In the evening plates of redcurrants and sugar were brought out – the grooms and boot-boys came to watch at the end of the day's work, and photographs were taken of the eleven as they came in after an innings. How important it all seemed, and the photographs looked at now, faded and discoloured, show round-faced and simple boys, who seemed to us then such mysterious and exciting beings.

Or, if ours was the visiting team, there was the drive back in the brake with its pair of horses after the match was over; two boys would sit on a box beside the coachman, and, sitting packed on the seats which faced each other, the rest of us crowded in – muslin dresses and white flannels – the boys wearing grey felt hats and the girls hats of straw with flowers. Trotting along the country roads, through the summer evenings, we broke into song to pass the time if the drive was long, and especially if our side had won. 'Shine, shine, moon, while I dance with Dinah dear', or 'Lousiana Lou', – 'dream, dream, dream of me, and I'll dream of you' we sang, and the villagers stopped to look at the turn-out rattling along and smile at its singing load.

CONSTANCE SITWELL *Bright Morning*

TENANTS'

BALLS

AND

CHRISTMAS

TREE

PARTIES

AT

NAWORTH

CASTLE

C. 1890–1900

THE balls were held in the great hall, with its stone floor overlaid by a temporary wooden one ... The band of twelve sat on the big oak table opposite the fireplace. The Hall was lit by huge chandeliers hanging from the roof trusses, each carrying forty-two candles, and round each corbel was a half chandelier with twenty-one ... They were all thickly festooned with chains of evergreens. So was the dais South wall, and some other parts. Gardeners and woodmen were at work for days on this lovely job.

All the food was cooked in the house. Refreshments, i.e. tea, coffee, lemonade, orangeade, stone ginger beer, cakes, biscuits, bunlets, and quarter oranges to suck, were served all night through in the Glen room. The magnificent cold suppers in regular 'sittings' were eaten in the billiard room – hams, turkeys, geese, beef, mutton, jellies, puddings, pastries, macedoine-of-fruit (not 'fruit salad' in those aristocratic days). Do children of all generations put away two, if not three suppers? We might sup, dance, doze on an empty sofa, at will. We danced a lot, with whoever would dance with us, and we were there to the finish. My mother never danced in my time, though she said she had loved it. My father danced the night through ... In my day the balls began at 8 or 8.30, and went on till 4.30 or 5. My mother said they used to go on longer – but I don't know how the candles could have lasted much more than ten hours. She said they had once gone on till 7. In later years I have been to two other families' 'Tenants' and 'Servants' balls. In both cases the Family left at midnight, 'when,' they said, 'the real ball begins.' I am dead certain that if our family, Parents and Young, had left at midnight, the 'real ball' would have ended. It was the kind of family and the kind of guests that made our presence essential to gaiety and good company ... The balls ended with 'Auld Lang Syne' sung in a huge running circle by everyone.

There were the exciting great Christmas Tree parties. The highest tree recorded was under the Dome at Castle Howard, 24 feet high ... My most constant memory is of the Naworth trees, twenty

(right) Lord Tredegar and parrot at a garden party at Tredegar Park, Monmouthshire, in the 1930s.

to twenty-three feet high. My mother was the moving spirit in all this. She bought vast quantities of toys for every boy and girl in every school on the estate and in Brampton. It was not 'one toy per child' but lashings over, to give a reasonable choice. They ranged from good concertinas to mouth organs; books to tin soldiers; paints, painting books, stories, tea-sets, tops, whips, hoops, skipping-ropes, dolls, dolls' beds made by 'Hop o' my Thumb' (John Hope, beloved joiner). My mother was in the midst of it all – hanging coloured glass balls of all shapes and sizes, and threading heavy red apples and oranges to weigh down the spruce branches. Our six boys, and the Bulkeley five (of Lanercost vicarage) took their share in creating the trees. Threaders hung apples and balls on rods. Hangers placed them on the tree. Artistic helpers made things: gold paper ships and stars. Needlewomen dressed dolls and upholstered cradles. We were an army of family, maids, governesses, vicar's wife, coachman's wife – anyone who liked a party came to sew, to gum gold and silver paper into massive chains, to decorate, and to place the scores of candles on the tree. From early days I claimed it as my privilege to dress the Fairy for the tree top.

DOROTHY HENLEY, *Rosalind Howard: Countess of Carlisle*

THE DUCHESS OF HAMILTON ENTERTAINS AT FERNE HOUSE 1931

At last we found ourselves marshalled into the drawing room, where a spindly Christmas tree stood decorated with tinsel toys and illuminated by coloured balls. Soon the village children from Berwick St John trooped in by invitation – fifty or sixty of them standing like a military unit. They had large heads, pale, weedy complexions, and goggle eyes. An overfat schoolmaster, crimson in the face, conducted a hymn while his minions sang with only a remote interest in the proceedings. The Duchess stood to attention surrounded by many ugly, grey-haired women, including a few deaf mutes. The village children, puny and unattractive, made a startling contrast to the healthy ducal offspring.

Her Grace then spoke a few words, welcoming the local children and giving them a dissertation on the advantages of country over city. Each leaf, she explained, was different in the country. There were many things to watch; they must appreciate and preserve its rustic joys.

One boy was asked the main difference between town and country and ruggedly replied, 'Oi think the moine difference is that in the cities there is so much dust and doirt and muck. In the country, the air is different and there are flewers.'

'Quite right, that is excellent.' The Duchess seemed a stalking crane in her off-white flannel skirt, socks and gym shoes. Finally she excoriated those who are cruel to the animals. 'Above all you must be kind to birds.'

The children were then encouraged to give bird calls for Father Christmas. They moved joylessly into the pitchpine panelled hall and intoned at the top of their melancholy screechy voices. After delays, and hitches and whispered commands from the family, and repeated shouts in unison from the children, Father Christmas materialised in the form of the Duke who was wheeled on to the scene by Geordie, his stalwart son. The Duke was dressed in red flannel with hood and a wig of white cotton wool. The children were told to line up in order of their ages. Those who were twelve years old must head the procession and be given a present.

A few mumbled words, then the village children were given orders to troop as a platoon into the frigid drawing-room. Each child took an orange and an apple from fruit-filled Tate sugar boxes placed near the door.

Everyone waited: grey-haired women, deaf mutes, refugee cats and dogs, and children of all ages. Then the lights went out; a few of the smaller village children began to whimper. The ducal grandchildren crawled in and out of the legs, human and animal, while outside the French windows their handsome parents could be seen for a flash or two, as they ran in the stormy darkness with matches and beacons. Suddenly a Catherine wheel hissed; then in the rain appeared a shower of 'golden rain'; squibs popped; jumping crackers exploded on the wet ground; chinese crackers went off in a series of half-hearted reports.

The whimpering village children now burst into screams of alarm. Terrified of the darkness and the noise, they howled, bellowed, shrieked with each new explosion. Babies cried, dogs barked, oranges and apples rolled on the floor. From exploding rockets blinding flashes revealed a maggot-crawling mass of panicking children and dogs. The hysteria reached a terrifying crescendo when a spurting, spluttering 'sparkler' came flying indoors.

CECIL BEATON, *The Wandering Years*

(right) The Princesses Louisa, Victoria and Maud on a visit to Sir William and Lady Armstrong at Cragside, 1884. From the water-colour by H. H. Emmison.

7
Royal
Visits

A royal visit has been the dream and night-mare of country-house owners from the Middle Ages up till the present day. What was the protocol? How could one avoid making some appalling bloomer? Where was the line between providing too much and too little? The stakes were especially high in the centuries before constitution-al monarchy, when the king or queen was the fount of jobs, honours and perquisites, and could make or mar the fortunes of a family.

In the sixteenth century Sir Nicholas Bacon ran up a new wing at his house at Gorhambury, in preparation for a visit by Queen Elizabeth; in the nineteenth century the de Murrieta family more than doubled the size of Wadhurst Park in Sussex, in order to entertain the Prince of Wales. In both

cases the visits took place. The unfortunate Sir Christopher Hatton turned Holdenby in Northamptonshire into a house the size of Chatsworth, in anticipation of putting up Queen Elizabeth. He ruined his estate, and she never came.

Others did not go so far, but most sizeable country houses had a suite of state rooms, one of the main functions of which was to provide for possible royal visits. The culminating feature of all such suites was a state bed, the more magnificent the better. In grand houses, even if the rest of the suite was sometimes used on other occasions, the bed was reserved for royalty. In some cases this meant that it was never slept in at all.

Then, at Wilton in 1779, the absurd situation arises of a state-bed being borrowed for a visit by George III and Queen Charlotte, who arrive with their own much more modest one. It is just about then, in fact, that one begins to notice a lack of fit between what hosts provide and royal guests desire. The latter are beginning to want to be treated more like ordinary mortals. The change becomes especially obvious in the account of Queen Victoria's visit to Stowe in 1845, as related by Elizabeth George, the daughter of a tenant farmer, who picked up the gossip from the Stowe servants.

Of course, there has always been a difference between a king or queen just looking in, as it were, for a hour or two, and coming for a night or a week, with an entourage, perhaps, of several hundred people. And visits from a Prince or Princess of Wales have tended to be more relaxed affairs; monarchy in embryo is less constricting than monarchy in fact.

Painting of Thomas Williams 'A Plasant Fool That Died In The Year 1687.' He was servant to Lord Coningsby, Hampton Court, Herefordshire.

EDWARD

III

FALLS

FOR

THE

COUNTESS

OF

SALISBURY

AT

WARK

CASTLE

1341

As soon as the lady knew of the king's coming, she set open the gates and came out so richly bedizened that every man marvelled of her beauty, and could not cease to regard her nobleness, with her great beauty and the gracious words and countenance that she made. When she came to the king she knelt down to the earth, thanking him of his succour and so led him into the castle to make him cheer and honour as she that could right well do it. Every man regarded her marvellously; the king himself could not withold his regarding of her, for he thought that he never saw before so noble nor so fair a lady; he was stricken therewith to the heart with a sparkle of fine love that endured long after; he thought no lady in the world so worthy to be beloved as she.

Thus they entered into the castle hand in hand; the lady led him first into the hall, and after into the chamber nobly apparelled. The king regarded so the lady that she was abashed; at last he went to a window to rest him, and so fell into a great study. The lady went about to make cheer to the lords and knights that were there, and commanded to dress the hall for dinner. When she had all devised and commanded them she came to the king with a merry cheer, (who was in a great study) and she said Dear Sir, why do you study so. . . . Then the king said, Dear lady, know for truth that since I entered into the castle there is a study come to my mind so that I can not choose but to muse, nor I can not tell what shall fall thereof; put it out of my heart I cannot . . . surely your sweet behaving, the perfect wisdom, the good grace, nobleness and excellent beauty that I see in you, hath so sore surprised my heart that I cannot but love you, and without your love I am but dead. Then the lady said, Right noble prince for God's sake mock nor tempt me not; I can not believe that it is true that you say, nor that so noble a prince as you be would think to dishonour me and my lord my husband, who is so valiant a knight.

. . . Therewith the lady departed from the king and went into the hall to have dinner; then she

Queen Elizabeth out hunting. Engraving from *The Book of Faulconrie* by George Turbeville (1575).

returned again to the king and brought some of his knights with her, and said, Sir, if it please you to come into the hall, your knights abideth for you to wash; you have been too long fasting. Then the king went into the hall and washed and sat down among his lords and the lady also. The king ate but little, he sat still musing, and as he did so cast his eye upon the lady . . . All that day the king tarried there and wyst not what to do. In the morning he arose and took leave of the lady saying, My dear lady to God I commend you till I return again, requiring you to advise you otherwise than you have said to me. Noble prince, quoth the lady, God the father glorious be your conduct, and put you out of all villain thoughts. Sir I am and ever shall be ready to do your grace service to your honour and to mine. Therewith the king departed all abashed.

FROISSART *Chronicles*

QUEEN

ELIZABETH

VISITS

LORD

HERTFORD

AT

ELVETHAM

1591

... **H**IS honor with all expedition set artificers a work, to the number of three hundred, many days before her Majesty's arrival, to enlarge his house with new rooms and offices ...

First there was made a room of estate for the Nobles, and at the end thereof a withdrawing place for her Majesty. The outsides of the walls were all covered with boughs, and clusters of ripe hazel nuts, the insides with arras, the roof of the place with works of ivy leaves, the floor with sweet herbs and green rushes.

Near adjoining unto this, were many offices new builded, as namely, Spicery, Lardery, Chandlery, Wine-cellar, Ewery, and Pantry: all which were tiled.

Not far off was erected a large hall, for the entertainment of Knights, Ladies and Gentlemen of chief account.

There was also a several place for her Majesty's footmen, and their friends.

Then there was a long bower for her Majesty's guard. Another for other servants of her Majesty's house. Another for my Lord's Steward, to keep his table in. Another for his Gentlemen that waited.

Most of these foresaid rooms were furnished with tables, and the tables carried twenty-three yards in length.

Moreover on the same hill there was raised a great common buttery. A Pitcher-house. A large Pastry, with five ovens new built, some of them fourteen feet deep. A great Kitchen, with four ranges, and a boiling place for small boiled meats. Another Kitchen, with a very long range, for the waste, to serve all comers. A Boiling-house, for the great boiler. A room for the Scullery. Another room for the Cook's lodgings. Some of these were covered with canvas, and other some with boards.

Between the Earl's house and the foresaid hill, where these rooms were raised, there had been made in the bottom, by handy labour, a goodly Pond, cut to the perfect figure of a half moon. In this Pond were three notable grounds, where hence to present her Majesty with sports and pastimes. The first was a *Ship Isle*, of a hundred foot in length, and four-score foot broad, bearing

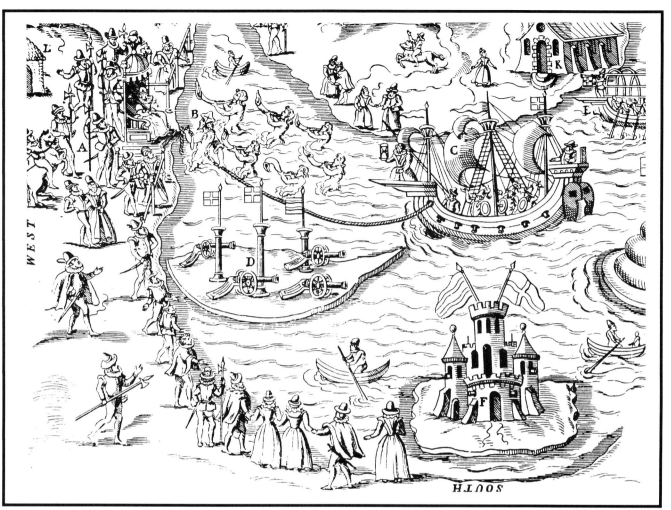

three trees orderly set for three masts. The second was a *Fort* twenty foot square every way, and overgrown with willows. The third and last was a *Snail Mount*, rising to four circles of green privy hedges, the whole in height twenty foot, and forty foot broad at the bottom. These three places were equally distant from the sides of the pond, and every one, by a just measured proportion, distant from the other. In the said water were divers boats prepared for music: but especially there was a pinnace, full furnished with masts, yards, sails, anchors, cables, and all other ordinary tackling, and with iron pieces; and lastly with flags, streamers, and pendants, to the number of twelve, all painted with divers colours and sundry devices.

Part of the Second Day's Entertainment

Presently after dinner, the Earl of Hertford caused a large canopy of estate to be set at the pond's head, for her Majesty to sit under, and to view some sports prepared in the water. The canopy was of green satin, lined with green taffeta sarcenet; every seam covered with a broad silver lace; valanced about, and fringed with green silk and silver, more than a hand-breadth in depth; supported by four silver pillars movable; and decked above head with four white plumes, spangled with silver. This canopy being upheld by four worthy knights (Sir Henry Grey, Sir Walter Hungerford, Sir James Marvin and Lord George Carew), and tapestry spread all about the pond's head, her Majesty, about four of the clock, came and sat under it, to expect the issue of some device, being advertised that there was some such thing towards.

At the further end of the pond, there was a bower, close built to the brink thereof; out of which there went a pompous array of sea persons, which waded breast-high or swam till they approached near the seat of her Majesty. Nereus, the Prophet of the Sea, attired in red silk, and having a cornered-cap on his curled head, did swim before the rest, as their pastor and guide. After him came

111

Queen Elizabeth's entertainment at Elvetham. Detail from an engraving of 1591.

the pond, all along the middle of the current, the Tritons sounded one half of the way; and then they ceasing, the cornets played their Scottish jigs. The melody was sweet, and the show stately.

JOHN NICHOLS, *Progresses of Queen Elizabeth*

ON Monday, [Aug 17, 1591] at eight of the clock in the morning, her Highness took horse, with all her train, and rode into the park: where was a delicate bower prepared, under the which her Highness's musicians played, and a crossbow by a Nymph, with a sweet song, delivered to her hands, to shoot at the deer, about some thirty in number, put into a paddock, of which number she killed three or four, and the Countess of Kildare one.

JOHN NICHOLS, *Progresses of Queen Elizabeth*

A

ROYAL

VISIT

1729

YESTERDAY the Queen and all the Royal Family dined at Claremont & I dined with the Duke and Sir Robert, &c. His Royal Highness came to us as soon as his and our dinner was over & drank a bumper of rack punch to the Queen's health which ye may be sure I devotedly pledged, & he was going on with another but Her Majesty sent in word that she was a going to walk in the garden, so that broke up the company. We walked till candle-light, being entertained with very fine french horns, then returned into his Great Hall, and everybody agreed that never was any thing finer lit. Her Majesty and Princess Charlotte, Lady Charlotte Roucy, Mr Shutz played there at quadrille, in the next room the Prince had the fiddlers and danced, and did me the honour to ask me if I could dance country dances, & told him yes, & if there had been a partner for me, I should have made one in that glorious company . . .

The Queen came from her cards to see that sight . . . there stood at the farther end of that room a table with bottles of wine for the dancers to drink.

PETER WENTWORTH TO LORD STRAFFORD, 21 AUGUST, 1729

five Tritons breast-high in the water, all with grisly heads, and beards of divers colours and fashions, and all five cheerfully sounding their trumpets. After them went two other Gods of the sea, Neptune and Oceanus, Phoreus and Glaucus, leading between them that pinnace whereof I spoke in the beginning of this treatise.

In the pinnace were three Virgins, which, with their cornets, played Scottish jigs, made three parts in one. There was also in the said pinnace another Nymph of the Sea, named Nedera, the old supposed love of Sylvanus, a God of the Woods. Near to her were placed three excellent voices, to sing to one lute, and in two other boas hard by, other lutes and voices, to answer by manner of echo. After the pinnace, and two other boats which were drawn after it by other sea-gods, the rest of the train followed breast-high in the water, all attired in scaly marine suits, and every one armed with a huge wooden squirt in his hand; to what end it shall appear hereafter. In their marching towards

Charles II being presented with a pineapple at an unidentified country house, c. 1675.

THE PRINCE OF WALES VISITS HARDWICK, 1619

The visit took place on August 9. The total cost was £91.13.2 (several thousand pounds in modern currency), mainly made up of presents to the royal entourage and to the servants of neighbours who sent gifts of food.

My Lord Darcy's man bringing a peacock	2s 0d
Sir William Kniveton's man bringing a fat cow	10s 0d
Mr Lee's man bringing fish and fowl	5s 0d
My Lady Stanhope's man bringing cheeses	2s 0d
Mr Bagshawe's man bringing powts	2s 0d
Sir Francis Wortley's man bring 2 rois	5s 0d
Mr Hunloke's bringing a calf	2s 0d
To Sir Thomas Momson's man bringing apples, apricocks, &c.	5s 0d
To the guard 6 pieces [a piecc = £1.3s.6d], to the footmen 2 pieces, to the waggoner a piece, to the yeoman of the cellar a piece, [yeoman of the] pantry a piece, [yeoman of the] ewery a piece, Butler a peice, master cook 4 pieces, yeoman cook a piece, yeoman of the pastry a piece, yeoman of the robes a piece, the saddler & helper a piece, Sir Francis Fullerton's man (cook) 11s 0d, to the waiter of the back stairs 11s 0d	£26.19.0d
To my Lady to play with the Prince at cards	£5.10.0
To John Bartram the London cook for himself, his workmen and a boy	£12.0.0
Given by my Lady to Mr Cave	£1.2.0
To the musicians that came from court	£2.4.0
More given to them playing at my Lady's chamber window	5s 0d
Mr Wright's man of Foston bringing a pannet of fish and fowl	5s 0d
To Mr Markham's man of Ollerton bringing half a stag	10s 0d
To my Lady which his honour gave away to the Prince's servants	£24.4.0
Wages paid to 15 several cooks employed at Hardwick at the Prince's coming	£13.5.8
Scullery labourers, turnspits, &c.	£3.15.6

ACCOUNT BOOK, 1ST EARL OF DEVONSHIRE

THE King dined in the new Dining Room, the Queen in the Cube Room; the Aide de Camp in the Breakfast Corner Room below stairs; Miss Herbert at which were Mrs Hegerdorn, the Queen's old Nurse, I believe, alias Mistress of the Robes, Her Majesty's Secretary and Comptroller Mr Harris, Ld Pembroke's Chaplain Dr & Mrs Eyre, in Lord Pembroke's old long dressing room over the Steward's Room; the Pages in the Coffee Room below Stairs; the Highlife below Stairs Gentry in the Stewards Room; the King's Footmen, Coachmen etc. in the Room over the Manège; & the rest of the Party-coloured Race in the Servants Hall, which will, I believe, give a good account of the eight Tables mentioned in the Papers sent to you by Lord Pembroke.

To accommodate their Majesties with a good Bed, I made interest with Mr Hill, Mr Beckford's Steward, to lend us his superb State Bed, which we brought to Wilton, slung on the Carriage of a Waggon, without the least damage, at no small expense, but what signifies money, when we were to entertain the Princes of the Land. I wish you had the list this Business cost, and His Majesty no worse, God Bless him, and I think you would not be very sorry. But it was necessary to get things decent and in order, and when we had bustled our hearts out for a week before the time, lo, and behold! when they arrived, they brought a snug double Tent Bed, had it put up in the Colonade Room, where the State Bed was already placed, in a crack, and slept, for any thing I know to the contrary, extremely quiet and well, directly under Ld & Lady Pembroke's & yr honour's Picture by Sir Joshua Reynolds.

The King dressed in the Hunting Room, where there was a fireplace made for the occasion, & now continues, and the Queen had the Corner Room for her Dressing Room, ornamented in the Toilette way, with Gold Candlesticks, & the Devil knows what which I cannot describe to you. The Blue Closet within was for her Majesty's private purposes, where there was a red new velvet Close Stool, and a very handsome China Jordan, which I had the honour to produce from an old collection, & you may be sure, I am as proud as Punch, that her Majesty condescended to piss in it.

DR EYRE TO LORD HERBERT, 1 JANUARY, 1779

PERHAPS you may have seen in the newspapers that our Fawley environs was then honour'd by the royal visitors. The servants at Fawley Court heard of them about two miles off; of course thought they were coming there, as they often did in his uncle's time, but to the no small disappointment of the nephew, as well as the domestics, they pass'd by, and went up to the Dowager Mrs Freeman's at Henley Park, not so noble a house, but all elegance, and one of the most beautiful situations imaginable. She most unluckily had been some time confined to her house with a violent cold; and the butler came running up to her dressing-room, saying, 'The King and Queen, M'am.' 'Don't alarm me, William' (you know her delicate manner); 'they are not coming here, but to Fawley Court, no doubt.' However, another footman followed immediately, saying the carriages were just driving up, and he had got a good fire in the drawing-room. She had only time to say, 'A smart breakfast, William,' and to throw on a huge cloak, and was down just as the King, Queen, two Princesses, Lady Louisa Clayton, and two gentlemen entered. They stayed two hours and a half, talked incessantly, seemed vastly pleased, and knew every family and their concerns in this neighbourhood, Mrs Freeman said, better than she did herself! The worst of these great visitors are that no servants must appear, and you are obliged to wait on them yourself; this, ill as she then felt, was very fatiguing; besides, not knowing the art, one must do it awkwardly. Mrs Freeman, after standing up in the corner to make the tea in the same spot, she handed a dish to her Majesty, and was carrying one to the Princess Royal, who laughingly said, 'I believe you forgot the King.' Mrs Freeman, in some agitation, was ready to laugh too, as she says she had at the moment completely forgotton that kings were to be served before ladies; but immediately rectified her mistake, and it was received in perfect good-humour; but what next vexed her sadly was that she had no opportunity of giving the least refreshment to Lady Louisa, the two gentlemen, who stood behind all the time, and were out so early in the morning, and to be at home so late, but she knew in the same room with their Majesties it was not to be attempted; therefore if you know of it, another breakfast is prepared in another room in case opportunity offers to let their attendants partake of it.

CAROLINE POWYS, *Letters*, 30 DECEMBER, 1785

THE PRINCE OF WALES IS JOVIAL AT HINCHINGBROKE 1789

At Christmas, 1789, His Royal Highness visited that bon vivant, the Earl of Sandwich, satirized by Churchill under the name of Jemmy Twitcher, at his seat at Hinchingbroke, where a numerous party annually assembled during the holidays. The mornings were devoted to concerts, at which his Royal Highness performed on the violincello; Madame Mara, then at the zenith of her ability, came from Burleigh with the Earl of Exeter to join the party; an excellent band, led by Ashley, was engaged, and his lordship assisted as usual on the kettledrums ... An elegant theatre was fitted up for the evening amusements, when *Love-à-la-Mode, the Mock Doctor, Virgin Unmasked, High Life below Stairs,* &c. were performed by amateurs; and an occasional prologue, written by his lordship in honour of his Royal Highness' visit, was spoken by L. Brown, Esq., M.P. for Huntingdonshire. After supper the evening concluded with catches and glees. His Royal Highness remained with the Earl one week, and on departing said, he had often heard of his lordship's hospitality, but could not have expected to have experienced so much gratification and pleasure in such a very numerous and diversified assemblage.

ROBERT HUISH, *Memoirs of George IV*

(below) Queen Victoria arriving at the railway station for a visit to Castle Howard, 1850.

(top right) The Prince of Wales at a shooting party at Elveden Hall, Suffolk, 1876.

(right) The Prince of Wales (second from left) at a meet before Easton Neston, Northamptonshire, October 1887.

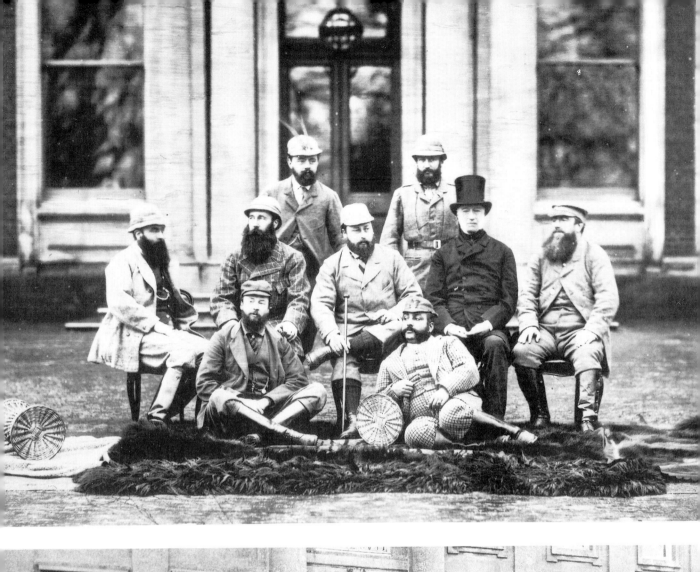

unbounded trouble to receive her Majesty with the greatest magnificence. Every part of his noble and vast mansion had been, in part, newly furnish'd and decorated, even articles that are generally made of cheap materials, and for the commonest every day wear – were of gold or silver if intended for the Queen's use.

Perhaps the Duke thought to surprise and gratify her Majesty by such delicate flattery, if so, he could hardly have been pleased when she said 'I am sure *I* have no such splendid apartments in either of my palaces' – considering who was the Speaker such an observation must be regarded as a very equivocal compliment.

The expensive and elaborate preparations were so evident that the very idea of having caused so serious an outlay must have been oppressive and unpleasant to her Majesty.

We were told that the Queen would have been far better pleased had her bedroom and dressing room been more simply furnished.

The head housemaid conducted the Royal pair to the apartments especially set apart for their private use, and she reported that the moment the Queen enter'd the bedroom she turn'd to the Prince and said 'O Albert, I know this carpet I have seen it before – it was offered to me, but I did not like to spend so much money on one carpet.' Then she told Mrs. Bennett to bring a drugget and lay over the carpet before she came to bed – adding 'I shall feel quite uncomfortable if it is not cover'd.'

DIARY OF ELIZABETH GEORGE

QUEEN VICTORIA IS SOUR AT STOWE 1845

AFTER hearing many details of the Royal visit, I cannot help thinking it was not quite satisfactory either to the Duke or his Guest. The Duke had been at great expense and had given himself

The Duchess of Teck descends the stairs of Trafford Park, near Manchester, with Sir Humphrey de Trafford, 1897. Behind her is her daughter Princess May, the future Queen Mary.
(top right) Prince Henry of Prussia shooting duck at Lyme Park, Cheshire, 1910.
(right) The Duke of York (later George V) out shooting at Elveden Hall, Suffolk, c. 1900.

AN

EMBARRASS-

ING

DOG

AT

HALTON

I was at Mr Alfred's first house-party when he opened Halton. The Prince of Wales was there, and Mr Alfred exhibited a number of small Japanese dogs, which had been taught to perform. Great confusion was aroused by the fact that, although the chief little dog performed, it was not according to the programme.

HALTON REMINISCENCES, 1880

THE

PRINCESS

OF

WALES

IS

STARTLED

WHEN the Princess of Wales, afterwards Queen Alexandra, visited Newstead, as the guest of the Duke and Duchess of St Albans at Bestwood, she was shown the haunted room, in which there was a cupboard let into the wall, with its door slightly ajar. Being always full of fun, H.R.H. said, 'I think the ghost must be in here,' and opened the cupboard door. Noticing a long curtain inside, she poked it with her parasol – and then drew back with a very startled '*Oh!*' For a faint scream came from behind the curtain and out rushed two housemaids, who had evidently hidden there to obtain a good view of the Royal visitor.

DUKE OF PORTLAND, *Men Women and Things*

119

The house is not identified; the dancer sounds like Margot Tennant, the future wife of H. H. Asquith.

THE Prince had a very keen sense of humour [but] he hated any of his friends made fun of; and, for example, was extremely displeased with a well-known peeress's sister because, when after some of her fantastic dancing, she playfully knelt before him and he smilingly said: 'Thank you, Lady Salome. Have you come to claim half of my Kingdom?' she replied – 'No, King Herod, but do give me Sir Ernest Cassel's head on a charger.'

JULIAN OSGOOD FIELD *Uncensored Recollections*

Queen Mary with Lord and Lady Lansdowne at Bowood House, Wiltshire, in 1922. (right) William Beckford's dwarf in front of Fonthill Abbey, Wiltshire.

8
Servants

*F*or at least five centuries complaining about their servants was one of the favourite pastimes of the English upper classes. The complaints have varied over the years. In the early centuries it was the treachery or disloyalty of upper servants that was the commonest theme. In those days upper servants were gentlemen or ladies by birth, often distantly related to the great people who employed them; they presided over lower echelons of yeomen or grooms, and acted as companions, agents, or business assistants to their employers, as well as playing cards or backgammon with them in the Great Chamber, or waiting on them at table. The opportunities for betraying vital secrets, setting husbands against wives or pushing their own interests were very great. In later centuries the status and social rank of upper servants changed, and the complaints changed too, to grumbles about drunkenness, slothfulness, unreliability or petty dishonesty, of the kind so brilliantly put across by Jonathan Swift, in his satirical *Directions to Servants.*

Such complaints went on into this century. But increasingly one gets the other side of the picture. Servants' own letters or memoirs begin to surface, and include their views of the gentry, not always complimentary ones. But of course there were endless variations in these teeming and highly stratified communities: there were loyal and loved servants, as well as dishonest or incompetent ones, kind and considerate employers, as well as cruel or aloof ones.

On the average, both size and ceremony decreased over the centuries. In late medieval and Tudor households, the ceremony involved in serving up meals is almost unbelievable. Even the minor business of supplying an earl with a bedside snack for the night involved ten servants in a ritual of bowing, kissing and processing all over the house. By the eighteenth century ritual had largely disappeared; but vestiges survived into Edwardian days, as in the dinner procession of upper servants from servants' hall to housekeeper's room. In general, the self-importance of upper servants derived from the fact that their predecessors had once been gentry.

At the Earl of Dorset's great house at Knole, 111 servants regularly sat down to dinner in the early seventeenth century. This was nothing out of the ordinary at the time, but by Edwardian days numbers even in the grandest houses seldom exceeded thirty or forty. The 1939–45 war was generally supposed to have dealt a death-blow to large staffs. But when the Earl of Derby's footman went berserk with a machine gun in 1952, one of the aspects of the drama which fascinated the public was that he drew coveys of servants out of the corridors and backstairs of Knowsley, on a scale which was thought to have gone for ever. As Winston Churchill is said to have remarked, 'It's nice to hear of a house where you can still get a left and right at a butler.'

(right) Musicians depicted in the frieze of the Great Chamber, Gilling Castle, North Yorkshire, c. 1585.

HOW

TO

GIVE

YOUR

MASTER

A

BATH

C. 1460

IF your sovereign will to the bath, his body to wash clean,
Hang sheets round about the roof. This is how I mean,
Every sheet full of flowers and herbs sweet and green,
And look you have sponges five or six, thereon to sit or lean.
Look there be a great sponge, thereon your sovereign to sit,
And on it a sheet, so he may bathe him there a fit,
Under his feet also a sponge, if there be any to put,
And always be sure of the door, and see that it is shut.
Take a basin in your hand full of hot herbs and fresh
And with a soft sponge in hand [start] his body to wash.
Rinse him with rose water warm and fair upon his flesh
Then let him go to bed, but see that it's sweet and nesh [soft]
But first set on his socks, his slippers on his feet,
That he may go fair to the fire, there to take his foot sheet,
Then with a clean cloth to wipe away all wet.
Then bring him to his bed, his troubles there to beat.

JOHN RUSSELL, *The Boke of Nurture*

The following ceremony involved four household departments, each of which had a yeoman in charge of it: the ewery, where linen, napkins, and basins and ewers for washing were kept; and the pantry, buttery, and cellar, which were responsible for bread, beer and wine respectively. The procession was marshalled by the usher of the chamber, assisted by attendant grooms. The earl is referred to as 'the Estate'. To 'give saye' means to give something to someone for trying out or tasting; it was a test of quality and precaution against poison.

BRINGING

UP

AN

EARL'S

'ALL-NIGHT'

C. 1500

THEN one of the grooms goeth into the ewery and calleth for all-night. The yeoman of the ewery giving him a towel, kisseth it and layeth it upon the groom's left shoulder, and after the basin and ewer with water (the groom giving him saye) then delivereth him a torch of wax lighted, if it be winter, and if it be not, unlighted. And so cometh he [the groom] to the pantry bar, where the yeoman usher with divers yeomen of the chamber do give attendance.

The bar put to, the usher calleth for all-night. The yeoman of the pantry bareheaded bringeth, in a napkin, one manchet and one cheate loaf, folded as one would wind it at the head and foot, laying the napkin plain over the one side. The usher giving him saye, and the said panter kissing the napkin and bread, the usher delivereth it to one of the yeomen and so goeth to the buttery bar, calling in like manner for all-night.

The yeoman of the buttery coming bareheaded bringeth the Estate's drinking cup covered, and a cup of saye, and a drinking cup for the Lady in like manner, and a great jug of silver covered all filled with beer. The usher, giving him saye of them all, after delivereth the said cups and jug to two other yeomen. Then he calleth for a cup of beer and so drinketh and giveth to all the servants in like manner. Then goeth he forth to the cellar (if the torch be lighted the groom [going] foremost with the torch and basin and ewer), so coming to the cellar bar in like manner calleth for all-night.

The yeoman of the cellar bringeth a cupboard cloth and a cup of state covered, and a cup of saye, and two great pots of wine, the usher giving him saye. If the torch be lighted the usher causeth the yeoman to kiss the cupboard cloth, and giveth it to the groom, laying it on his left shoulder, and giveth the two pots to one other yeoman, and taketh in his own hand the cup of state with the cup of saye: the torchlight foremost, the usher next, the bread next to him, the beer cup for the Estate next him, the cup of beer next and last the wine pots.

In this manner they go to the bedchamber. If the torch be not lighted then he with the torch and basin goeth behind last, and the usher foremost with the cupboard cloth on his right shoulder. Coming to the cupboard, the usher making curtsey, the torch standing at the nether end of the cupboard, and the chamberer being ready taketh the light off the cupboard and standing at the upper and holdeth the same in her hand. The usher, setting down the cup of state upon the cupboard [and] kissing the cupboard cloth, spreadeth it abroad upon the cupboard. If the groom has the cupboard cloth then he kisseth it. Then he [the usher] taketh the bread of the yeoman, he kissing it. So unfolding the napkin, foldeth it plain, setting the bread in it, and giveth saye thereof to the yeoman. Then he covereth the bread with the one end of the napkin, so setteth it at the upper end of the cupboard.

Then, taking the Estate's drinking cups, giving the yeoman sayes, he setteth them next the bread; then the jug of beer, setting it next the cups; then the pots of wine, giving sayes, setteth them next the jugs; and then he taketh the towel from the shoulder of the groom, kissing it, and raiseth it upon his own left shoulder, and giveth saye to the groom of the water. Then setteth last the basin and ewer down, and kissing the towel layeth it upon the ewer.

Then he uncovereth the Estate's cup, setting it and the cup of saye covered in the middle of the cupboard, most to the over end. Then taketh the wax light from the chamberer and setteth it upon the cupboard. And so all with curtsies depart and avoid the chamber. Then the usher of the chamber giveth charge of the cupboard to one of the gentlewomen of presence, if the Lady lieth with the Estate, or else one of the grooms hath the charge.

HARLEIAN MSS, ORDERS OF SERVICE BELONGING TO THE DEGREE OF AN EARL

(left) Bradford table cloth, early seventeenth century, from Weston Park.

TABLE SEATING
The Household Of The Earl Of Dorset At Knole, In Kent, 1613–24

At My Lord's Table

My Lord
My Lady Margaret
Mr. Sackville
John Musgrave

My Lady
My Lady Isabella
Mr. Frost
Thomas Garret

At The Parlour Table

Mrs. Field
Mrs. Grimsditch
Mrs. Fletcher
Mrs. Willoughby
Mrs. Stewkly
Mrs. Wood
Mr. Dupper, Chaplain
Mr. Matthew Caldicott, my
    Lord's favourite
Mr. Edward Legge, Steward
Mr. Peter Basket, Gentleman of
    the Horse
Mr. Marsh, Attendant on my
    Lady

Mr. Wooldridge
Mr. Cheyney
Mr. Duck, Page
Mr. Josiah Cooper, a
Frenchman, Page
Mr. John Belgrave, Page
Mr. Billingsley
Mr. Graverner, Gentleman
Usher
Mr. Marshall, Auditor
Mr. Edwards, Secretary
Mr. Drake, Attendant

At The Clerks' Table In The Hall

Edward Fulks and John
    Edwards, Clerks of the
Kitchen
Edward Care, Master Cook
William Smith, Yeoman of the
    Buttery
Henry Keble, Yeoman of the
    Pantry
John Mitchell, Pastryman
Thomas Vinson, Cook
John Elnor, Cook
Ralph Hussie, Cook
John Avery, Usher of the Hall
Robert Elnor, Slaughterman

Benjamin Staples, Groom of the
    Great Chamber
Thomas Petley, Brewer
William Turner, Baker
Francis Steeling, Gardener
Richard Wicking, Gardener
Thomas Clements, Under
    Brewer
Samuel Vans, Caterer
Edward Small, Groom of the
    Wardrobe
Samuel Southern, Under Baker
Lowry, a French boy

The Nursery

Nurse Carpenter
Jane Sisley

Widow Ben
Dorothy Pickenden

At The Long Table In The Hall

Robert Care, Attendant on my Lord

Mr. Gray, Attendant likewise

Mr. Rogert Cook, Attendant on my Lady Margaret

Mr. Adam Bradford, Barber

Mr. John Guy, Groom of my Lord's Bedchamber

Walter Comestone, Attendant on my Lady

Edward Lane, Scrivener

Mr. Thomas Poor, Yeoman of the Wardrobe

Mr. Thomas Leonard, Master Huntsman

Mr. Woodgate, Yeoman of the Great Chamber

John Hall, Falconer

James Flennel, Yeoman of the Granary

Rawlinson, Armourer

Moses Shonk, Coachman

Anthony Ashly, Groom of the Great Horse

Griffin Edwards, Groom of my Lady's Horse

Francis Turner, Groom of the Great Horse

William Grynes,   ″   ″

Acton Curvett, Chief Footman

The Armourer's Man

Ralph Wise, his Servant

John Swift, the Porter's Man

James Loveall, Footman

Sampson Ashley,   ″

William Petley,   ″

Nicholas James,   ″

Paschal Beard,   ″

Elias Thomas,   ″

Henry Spencer, Farrier

Edward Goodsall

John Sant, the Steward's Man

Ralph Wise, Groom of the Stables

Thomas Petley, Under Farrier

John Stephens, The Chaplain's Man

John Haite, Groom for the Stranger's Horse

Thomas Giles, Groom of the Stables

Richard Thomas, Groom of the Hall

Christopher Wood, Groom of the Pantry

George Owen, Huntsman

George Vigeon,   ″

Thomas Grittan, Groom of the Buttery

Solomon, the Bird-Catcher

Richard Thornton, the Coachman's Man

Richard Pickenden, Postillion

William Roberts, Groom

John Atkins } Men to
Clement Doory } carry wood

The Laundry-Maids' Table

Mrs. Judith Simpton

Mrs. Grace Simpton

Penelope Tutty, the Lady Margaret's Maid

Anne Mills, Dairy-Maid

Prudence Butcher

Anne Howse

Faith Husband

Elinor Thompson

Goodwife Burton

Grace Robinson, a Blackamoor

Goodwife Small

William Lewis, Porter

The Kitchen And Scullery

Diggory Dyer

Marfidy Snipt

John Watson

Thomas Harman

Thomas Johnson

John Morockoe, a Blackamoor

LADY

WILLOUGHBY

SPEAKS

HER

MIND

TO

A

SERVANT

1594

THOU hast used thy pleasure in bad speeches of the Countess of Shrewsbury, and Mr Thomas Spencer's wife, and others. Thou hast practised dissensions betwixt my husband and me from the beginning. Thou hast set my father and him at jars, because thou mightest the better fish and enrich thyself, as thou hast done, with their spoils. Thou wouldst (being in thy house) have married me to thy cousin Cludd, a poor cozening knave of my father's, that came lousy to him, and theretofore in thy heart couldst never since abide me, tho' hitherto I have concealed it.

I was once before for thy pleasure and persuasions little better than hurled out of this house [Midleton Hall, Warwickshire], being great bellied, when thou didst hope both by that means might have perished.

... And notwithstanding all this and much worse than this, thy ordinary protestation is by the faith of an honest man. Malicious knave thou art that canst not spare poor gentlewomen and infants with thy tongue and practices; gentleman thou know'st thyself to be none, and tho' at this instant I have no better means of revenge than a little ink and paper, let thy soul and carcass be assured to bear and taste of these injuries in other sort and terms than from and by the hands of a woman.

BRIDGET, LADY WILLOUGHBY, TO CLEMENT FISHER, 1594

TIPS

ABOUT

SERVANTS

FROM

SIR

WILLIAM

WENTWORTH

1604

FOR servants be very careful to keep only those that be born of good and honest friends and be well willing, humble, diligent and honest. Take heed what you speak before them, if you be wise, especially touching any great person ... Yet in any case trust them not more than you needs must in matters that may greatly concern your danger. For almost all treacheries have been wrought by servants and the final end of their service is gain and advancement,

Col. Pl. X (right) Servants at Tichborne House, Hampshire. Detail from the painting of the distribution of the Tichborne Dole. Gillis van Tilborch, 1670.

Col. Pl. XI–XIV Gardeners at Hartwell House, Buckinghamshire. Details from the paintings by Balthasar Nebot, 1738.

Col. Pl. XV Killing flies at Dynes Hall, Essex. Diana Sperling, c.1815–20.

which, offered by any to them that wants it and longs for it, brings a dangerous temptation. Only some ancient honest servants of your father's whose wealth and credit depend most upon your house and are seated on your ground are like to be fast and true to you than other hirelings &c. Yet build no judgement upon things they speak, though they be honest; for ordinarily such men do mistake and misreport matters for want of learning and sounder judgment, though they be honest and mean truth.

SIR WILLIAM WENTWORTH OF WENTWORTH WOODHOUSE

DUTIES

OF

A

TRUMPETER

1610

WHEN the Earl is to ride a journey, he is early every morning to sound, to give warning, that the officers may have time to make all things ready for breakfast and the grooms of the stable to dress and meat the horses. When it is breakfast time, he is to make his second sounding: breakfast ended, and things in a readiness, he is to sound the third time, to call to horse. He is to ride foremost, both out and into any town, sounding his trumpet. Upon the way he may sound for pleasure. But if he see the day so spent that they are like to bring late to their lodging, he is to sound the tantara, to move them to hasten their pace . . . He and the Drummer are to go often into the stable, to acquaint the horses with the sound of the trumpet, and the noise of the drum.

ROBERT BAINBRIDGE, *Some Rules and Orders for the Government of the House of an Earle*

Serving an al fresco meal to Queen Elizabeth, from an engraving of *c.*1570 from *The Book of Faulconrie* by George Turbeville (1575).

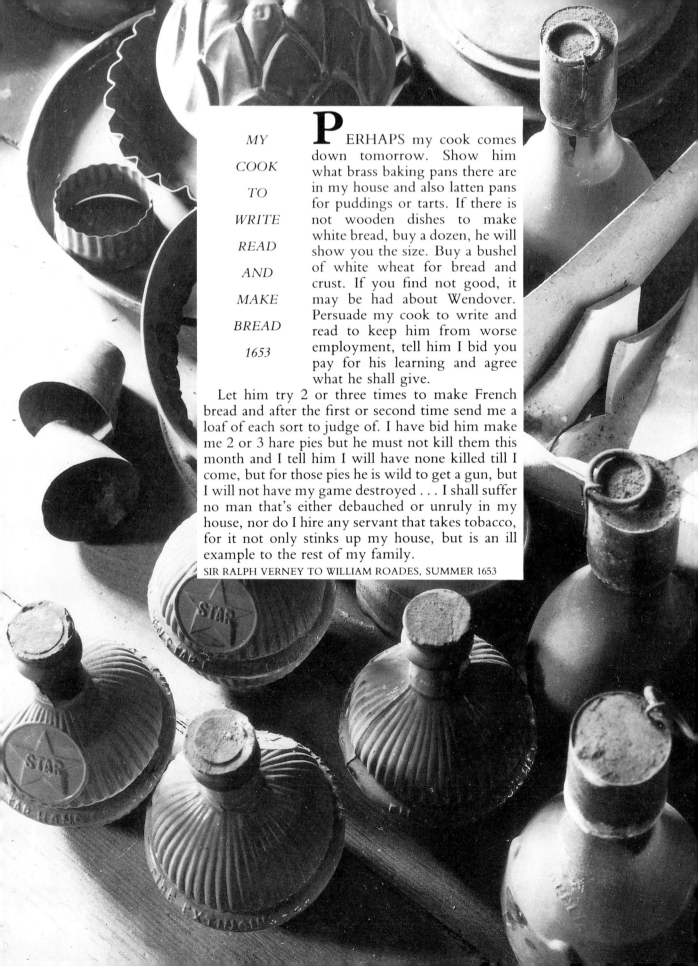

MY

COOK

TO

WRITE

READ

AND

MAKE

BREAD

1653

PERHAPS my cook comes down tomorrow. Show him what brass baking pans there are in my house and also latten pans for puddings or tarts. If there is not wooden dishes to make white bread, buy a dozen, he will show you the size. Buy a bushel of white wheat for bread and crust. If you find not good, it may be had about Wendover. Persuade my cook to write and read to keep him from worse employment, tell him I bid you pay for his learning and agree what he shall give.

Let him try 2 or three times to make French bread and after the first or second time send me a loaf of each sort to judge of. I have bid him make me 2 or 3 hare pies but he must not kill them this month and I tell him I will have none killed till I come, but for those pies he is wild to get a gun, but I will not have my game destroyed . . . I shall suffer no man that's either debauched or unruly in my house, nor do I hire any servant that takes tobacco, for it not only stinks up my house, but is an ill example to the rest of my family.

SIR RALPH VERNEY TO WILLIAM ROADES, SUMMER 1653

Schedule For The Housekeeper And Others At Bank Hall, 1677

Mondays – look out the foul cloths and call the maids and sit or stay by them till they be all mended.

Tuesdays – clean the rooms, and chairs from the great room to the nursery and the beds on the top and bottom; and dust the feathers.

Wednesdays – clean all the rooms, chairs and beds under and top with the feathers, from the nursery to the Eagle Chamber.

Thursdays – clean the hall and parlours, windows, tables, chairs and pictures below stairs.

Fridays – scour all the grates tongs and hand-irons.

Saturdays – clean the store house shelves and dressers.

Every day – once for one hour in the forenoon go through all the rooms and see it doth not rain into them and dust them all down; and sweep them.

Dairy maid – wash your dairy every day; and for your milk and butter do as you will be directed; Churn – Tuesdays and Fridays. Serve the swine and poultry night and morning; and for the hogsmeat any of the servant men shall carry them out for you. Observe well the time for setting out all sorts of your poultry, once every week make the house bread; and same shall help you to knead. To help them wash when washing day comes; Milk your cows in good time.

Cook maid – wash your kitchen every night, and the Larders every other day, shelfs and dressers and scour the pewter we use every Friday night, and all the rest of the pewter once every month. Keep your Kitchen extraordinary clean. To help upon washing days the rest of the maids to wash. And make all the maids bring down their candle-sticks first thing in a morning to be made clean.

REGULATION FOR THE HOUSEHOLD OF THE MOORE FAMILY, BANK HALL, NEAR LIVERPOOL

Design for an unidentified country-house kitchen, by William Kent, c. 1730.

LADY

JUDITH

LOOKS

FOR

A

CHAMBER

MAID

C. 1704

PRAY inquire for a Chamber Maid for us, & that you may fully acquaint her with our business I have sent you an account of what it is that we expect from her. First, she must work plain work very well, Sr. Ab: wears very fine linen & she must make & mend for him & me & for my son & sister, she must wash & smooth all the fine linens & muslins & dress our heads, & keep our chambers neat & clean, & do all that belongs to the Chamber maid's place. The Dairy maid, when her cows are milked, the poultry & swine fed & done the business that belongs to her Dairy, shall help her wash, & likewise to help her to wash that part of the house that is not in constant use; but our Lodging Chambers that we lie in every night, she must do them by herself. We would not have a young raw finical Lass, for then she will mind nothing so much as the dressing up of herself, but a plain discreet staid servant, one that has been used to such business & is able to perform it. If you can hear of such an one for us, that will undertake to do this,

we shall think our selves much oblig'd to you for your endeavours herein.

LETTER FROM LADY JUDITH DANBY, OF SWINTON HALL, YORKSHIRE

vants being allowed to go into the cellar with them but the under butler only.

HOUSEHOLD ORDERS OF THE DUKE OF CHANDOS FOR CANNONS, IN MIDDLESEX

DUCAL WELCOME AT CANNONS 1721 . . .

SEPTEMBER 11, 1721. For the future all Gentlemen's Livery Servants that come to the house be taken into the cellar by the Under Butler and have there one horn of strong beer or ale given to each of them and if their masters dine here that this be done after dinner, none of his Grace's ser-

. . . and lack of it at Welbeck, c.1769 We Your Grace's servants whose names are here enclosed beg leave to petition for ale; not for ourselves particular, but for the servants of Your Grace's friends, which we have been frequently refused by Mr Martin, Your Grace's butler, without giving any reason for the same, but in saying I am Master and you shall have none.

PETITION TO THE DUKE OF PORTLAND, WELBECK ABBEY, NOTTINGHAMSHIRE

The kitchen in the Nostell Priory doll's house, c. 1740.

then take care to fill them up again with clean water, that you may not lessen your master's liquor.

That the salt may lie smooth in the salt-cellar, press it down with your moist palm.

When a gentleman is going away after dining with your master, be sure to stand full in his view, and follow him to the door, and as you have opportunity look full in his face, perhaps it may bring you a shilling; but if the gentleman has lain there a night, get the cook, the housemaid, the stable-men, the scullion, and the gardener, to accompany you, and to stand in his way to the hall in a line on each side him: If the gentleman performs handsomely, it will do him honour, and cost your master nothing.

You need not wipe your knife to cut bread from the table, because, in cutting a slice or two it will wipe itself.

JONATHAN SWIFT, *Directions to Servants*

'Lucy' had retired to Warwickshire because Byron had made her pregnant. The gap after 'the Girls on the Manor' is due to an excision made by Thomas Moore, Byron's editor; the original letter does not survive.

DEAN

SWIFT

ON

A

BUTLER'S

DUTIES

1745

IF an humble companion, a chaplain, a tutor, or a dependent cousin happen to be at table, whom you find to be little regarded by the master, and the company, which no body is readier to discover and observe than we servants, it must be the business of you and the footman, to follow the example of your betters, by treating him many degrees worse than any of the rest; and you cannot please your master better, or at least your lady.

If any one calls for small-beer towards the end of dinner, do not give yourself the pains of going down to the cellar, but gather the droppings and leavings out of the several cups, and glasses, and salvers onto one; but turn your back to the company, for fear of being observed.

When you clean your plate, leave the whiting plainly to be seen in all the chinks, for fear your lady should believe you have not cleaned it.

If you are curious to taste some of your master's choice bottles, empty as many of them just below the neck as will make the quantity you want; but

LORD

BYRON

IMPROVES

HIS

FEMALE

STAFF

1811

I am plucking up my spirits, and have begun to gather my little sensual comforts together. Lucy is extracted from Warwickshire; some very bad faces have been warned off the premises, and more promising substituted in their stead; the partridges are plentiful, hares fairish, pheasants not quite so good, and the Girls on the Manor . . . . Just as I had formed a tolerable establishment my travels commenced, and on my return I found all to do over again; my former flock were all scattered; some married, not before it was needful. As I am a great disciplinarian, I have just issued an edict for the abolition of caps; no hair to be cut on any pretext; stays permitted, but not too low before; full uniform always in the evening; Lucinda to be commander – *vice* the present, about to be wedded (*mem*, she is 35 with a flat face and a squeaking voice), of all the makers and unmakers of beds in the household.

BYRON TO FRANCES HODGSON, 25 SEPTEMBER, 1811

Servants of the Drummond family, at Denham, Buckinghamshire, as drawn by one of the Drummond children, c. 1830.

WHILE waiting at dinner, never be picking your nose, or scratching your head, or any other part of your body; neither blow your nose in the room; if you have a cold, and cannot help doing it, do it on the outside of the door; but do not sound your nose like a trumpet, that all the house may hear when you blow it; still it is better to blow your nose when it requires, than to be picking it and snuffing up the *mucus*, which is a filthy trick. Do not yawn or gape, or even sneeze, if you can avoid it; and as to hawking and spitting, the name of such a thing is enough to forbid it, without a command. When you are standing behind a person, to be ready to change the plates, &c., do not put your hands on the back of the chair, as it is very improper; though I have seen some not only do so, but even beat a kind of tune upon it with their fingers. Instead of this, stand upright with your hands hanging down or before you, but not folded. Let your demeanour be such as becomes the situation which you are in. Be well dressed, and have light shoes that make no noise, your face and hands well washed, your finger-nails cut short and kept quite clean underneath; have a nail-brush for that purpose, as it is a disgusting thing to see black dirt under the nails. Let the lapels of your coat be buttoned, as they will only be flying in your way.

T. COSNETT, *Footman's Directory*

NO wine was ever served at dinner, though this did not touch me, as at that time I drank nothing. Water, drunk out of black glass, was the family beverage. Nevertheless, the butler and his pantry cronies appeared to indulge freely in wine! In that way it was hardly possible to find a more drunken establishment; Hesleyside was simply a house of public refreshment for the neighbourhood and, I am sorry to say, remained so when William and I later had it to ourselves. Mauxwell, the butler, a sober enough man himself, gave drink out, he said, for the honour of the family! And my poor husband, who

laboured latterly for the effervescent popularity of the lower orders, well knew that drink was a high road to their hearts. How mercilessly was his mistaken generosity taken advantage of! Most certainly Hesleyside in those days was a rum and disorderly establishment.

There was a still in the garden-shed for the distillation of mint, as was the custom in old-fashioned gardens, and which, as far as we knew, was used for no other purpose. But in Hodgson's time as gardener this was not the case. It was in the days of home-brewing, and the brewing refuse was always thrown to the pigs. Hodgson, however, begged it from his unsuspecting master for the raising of carrots, which did not thrive in the Hesleyside garden soil, and had to be bought. Some fine carrots were duly produced as evidence of what a manufactured soil could do, although in reality they had been introduced from outside. For Hodgson was using the refuse for the distillation of something a good deal more potent than peppermint, and the inmates of the saddle-room were in the secret with him.

L.E.O. CHARLTON, *Memoirs of a Northumbrian Lady*

PROTOCOL

AMONG

UPPER

SERVANTS

AT

HENHAM

HALL

SUFFOLK

C. 1870

ANOTHER of our amusements was to hide and watch the upper servants march from the servant's hall to 'The Room' [the housekeeper's room]; this was a serious ceremony: the butler and housekeeper and lady's maid had their meat course in 'the hall', the butler carving whilst the hall-boy waited. When the sweets were handed, the upper servants rose from the table each carrying a plate of pudding in one hand and a glass of beer in the other, and walked majestically out of the room in single file, according to the rank of their master or mistress.

The ladies' maids and valets were always addressed amongst themselves by the name of their employers. A friend of mine arrived late at a country house and as he was hurriedly changing into his evening clothes he heard a valet call to the lady's maid in the next room: 'Hurry up, Ripon, you'll be late for supper, both the Abercorns are down.'

LADY AUGUSTA FANE, *Chit-Chat*

POWDERING

NO

FUN

C. 1890

POWDER money used to be allowed in some houses, while in others the powder itself was provided and was always of the best. Footmen of the younger generation should be thankful that this daily powdering of the hair has gone out of fashion, for it was indeed a very unpleasant business. After the hair had been moistened, soap was put on and rubbed into a stiff lather, and the combing was done so that the teeth marks would show evenly all over. Powder was then applied with a puff and the wet mass allowed to dry on the head until it became quite firm. In the evening the hair was always to be washed and oiled to prevent its becoming almost fox colour, and I remember I was hardly ever free from colds in houses where this hair-powdering was the regulation.

JOHN JAMES, *Memories of a House Steward*

ORDER

OF

LIVERIES

1900

LIVERIES are given 1st April and 1st October of each year. Evening Liveries every Twelve Months. Tweed Jackets every Twelve Months (except the Hall Porter and Steward's Room Boy, they have a Tweed Suit). Hats, Gloves, and Stockings every Six Months, except on special occasions, such as Drawing Rooms, Weddings, etc. Orders for Gloves and Stockings for them will be issued from time to time as required. Macintoshes are given according to wear.

When Evening Liveries have been worn Six Months from date of entry into service, the wearer is entitled to a New Suit on the 1st of April prox. If within Six Months the wearer is not entitled to a New Suit until the following April. When Morning Liveries have been worn Three Months from date of entry, the wearer is entitled to a New Suit either in April or October, according to date of entry, but if not worn Three Months the wearer is not entitled to a Suit until the next term, or issue of Liveries.

Overcoats have to be worn Twelve Months before the wearer is entitled to another on the aforesaid date, 1st of April.

The same rule applies to giving up Liveries on leaving service. Within the above periods they are

Maid in the basement corridor at Stowe House, Buckinghamshire. By J.C. Nattes, 1807.

Lord Salisbury's property, over those periods they are the wearer's property.

Stable Liveries are given and retained on the same system.

HOUSEHOLD REGULATIONS FOR HATFIELD HOUSE, 1900

MEMORIES

OF

BELVOIR

CASTLE

1905

THE gong man was an old retainer, one of those numberless ranks of domestic servants which have completely disappeared and today seem fabulous. He was admittedly very old. He wore a white beard to his waist. Three times a day he rang the gong – for luncheon, for dressing-time, for dinner. He would walk down the interminable passages, his livery hanging a little loosely on his bent old bones, clutching his gong with one hand and with the other feebly brandishing the padded-knobbed stick with which he struck it. Every corridor had to be warned and the towers too, so I suppose he banged on and off for ten minutes, thrice daily.

Then there were the lamp-and-candle men, at least three of them, for there was no other form of lighting. Gas was despised, I forget why – vulgar, I think. They polished and scraped the wax off the candelabra, cut wicks, poured paraffin oil, and unblackened glass chimneys all day long. After dark they were busy turning wicks up or down, snuffing candles, and dewaxing extinguishers. It was not a department we liked much to visit. It smelt disgusting and the lampmen were too busy. But the upholsterer's room was a great treat. He was exactly like a Hans Andersen tailor. Cross-legged he sat in a tremendous confusion of curtains and covers, fringes, buttons, rags and carpets, bolsters, scraps (that could be begged off him), huge curved needles like scimitars, bodkins, hunks of beeswax to strengthen thread, and hundreds of flags. The flags on the towertop, I suppose, got punished by the winds and were constantly in need of repair. I never saw him actually at work on anything else. There were slim flags for wind, little ones for rain, huge ones for sunshine, hunting flags, and many others.

The water-men are difficult to believe in today. They seemed to me to belong to another clay.

Servants at Erddig Hall, Denbighshire, in the late nineteenth century: William Hughes, woodman, William Gittus, foreman carpenter, Jane Brown, housekeeper, and an unidentified gamekeeper, with his son.

They were the biggest people I had ever seen, much bigger than any of the men of the family, who were remarkable for their height. They had stubbly beards and a general Bill Sikes appearance. They wore brown clothes, no collars, and thick green baize aprons from chin to knee. On their shoulders they carried a wooden yoke from which hung two gigantic cans of water. They moved on a perpetual round. Above the ground floor there was not a drop of hot water and not one bath, so their job was to keep all jugs, cans, and kettles full in the bedrooms, and morning or evening to bring the hot water for the hip-baths. We were always a little frightened of the water-men. They seemed of another element and never spoke but one word, 'Water-man', to account for themselves.

LADY DIANA COOPER, *The Rainbow comes and goes*

TROUBLES

OF

A

FOOTMAN

1910

NOW it was while I was at this place in Devon that I met the girl who was to become my wife. She was then head kitchen-maid and in her pale blue uniform she looked so lovely that I fell in love with her. This was all right, but courting while in service was then strictly forbidden. We hadn't to be seen talking, so we used to leave notes under the lamp room mat; or we'd get up at four in the morning and slip out for a walk in the woods. I saved up for a ring (and on £26 a year that took some doing), though I knew very well that Nellie must never be seen wearing it. I think it mostly got worn in those days between four and nine in the morning. It was sometimes possible for us to meet secretly outside for a few minutes in the evening and neither of us will ever forget the time when Nellie, having as usual nipped out of the larder window, went to cross a five-foot plank which the builders had left to cover a trench. It had been a very wet day and what wasn't water in that trench was wet clay and sloshy mud. Nellie (in pale blue) slipped in and I'd a devil of a tug o' war with the mud before it would let her go. Of course this spoilt our little evening's courtship.

MEMORIES OF GERALD HORNE

LAMENT

OF

A

LAUNDRY-

MAID

1911

THERE are 22 servants in the house, of course that does not include those who come into work every day. There is a man in the kitchen who works all the meat (the butcher he is called). He prepares all the meat. Then there is a man in the scullery, also a woman kept for washing up, and two stillroom maids, and a woman comes every day to bake the bread. So there are five in the kitchen and two regularly in the scullery. I am afraid Miss Brown that sounds very much like a fairy tale, but when I tell you there are fourteen cold meats sent up every day for my Lord's luncheon including four or five hot dishes, you will understand there is some work to be done in the kitchen alone! Then my Lord has a clean table cloth for every meal. Is it not ridiculous? Sometimes when he is alone we have twenty three table clothes in the wash in a week and when he has a lot of company we have anywhere from thirty six to forty. His sister is Lady Hereford of Ludlow, and when she and her daughters come here there is plenty of work for everyone. The sideboard cloths are changed three or four times a week and my Lord has a clean cloth, on every tray

taken up to him. I often say if cleanliness would keep any one alive, then Viscount Tredegar would never die.

LORD ASTOR'S BUTLER C. 1930

YET Mr Lee could be unexpectedly kind. At a dinner there was once nearly a disaster which could have turned into a social scandal. A public figure of some standing was talking to Lady Astor as a footman was serving him. 'I need a skivvy for my kitchen, can any of your servants recommend one, do you think?'

Give her ladyship her due, she tried to temper his speech. 'What kind of servant do you want?'

'Oh, any little slut will do.' The footman stepped back and went white as a sheet. 'I had some sort of sixth sense that things weren't what they should be with him,' Mr Lee told me. 'I moved over as quickly as I could and caught him just as he was about to pour the hot sauce over the guest's head. There was no doubt about it, he told me that was what he was going to do when I got him outside.'

Mr Lee didn't so much as reprimand him when he'd heard his story. He didn't say a word; he went to his sideboard, poured a glass of port, handed it to the footman, patted him on the back and said, 'Come back in when you feel you can.' Mr Lee saw Lady Astor the following day and complained of her guest's conversation. 'He had no right to

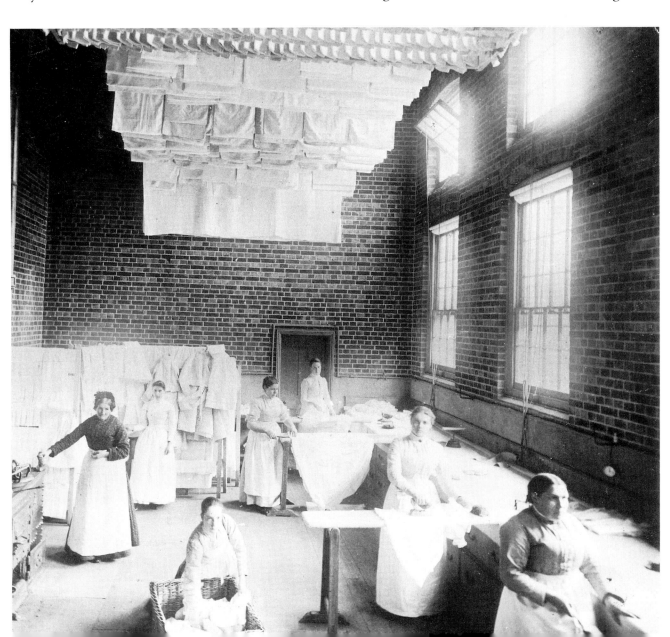

speak like that about servants, even behind their backs, my lady, and in our hearing, it's unforgivable.' He didn't mention the footman's reaction to what had been said.

'You're quite right, Lee, and that man will never visit us again.' She asked for the footman to be sent to see her, and she apologized to him.

ROSINA HARRISON, *Rose: my life in service*

Henry Moate, butler to Sir George Sitwell at Renishaw Hall, Derbyshire. C. R. W. Nevinson, 1918, detail.

(left) The laundry at Petworth House, Sussex, c. 1890.

REDUCTION OF STAFF AT KNOWSLEY 1952

ON October 7, when at Hoylake, Winstanley [Harold Winstanley, footman to the Earl of Derby at Knowsley, in Lancashire] bought a Schmeisser gun and some hundreds of rounds of ammunition from a friend for a pair of trousers and £3. On November 5, about 8.15 a.m., Lady Derby was sitting in the smoking-room having dinner. Behind her was a door to the second library. About 8.15 the door from the first library opened and there stood Winstanley. The first thing that Lady Derby noticed was that he was smoking a cigarette. She rose from her chair and faced him, and then saw that he was holding a gun which was pointed directly at her. He told her to turn round and she did so and immediately the gun fired. Lady Derby felt a blow on her neck. She fell forward with the force of it.

Lady Derby could hear Winstanley moving about behind her. She kept still, and that may have saved her life. A few moments or a few minutes later she heard Stallard, the butler, say: 'Harold.' Immediately there was a burst of fire and she felt a thud as he fell.

The suspense went on and she could hear Winstanley moving about the room. She heard someone say: 'No,' and that was followed by two bursts of fire and then all was quiet. That no doubt was Stuart, the under-butler. The next thing Lady Derby knew was that she was being attended to by her maid ...

Having finished in the smoke-room and library, Winstanley walked out into the inner hall, and he there saw Sullivan, Lord Derby's valet, halfway down the stairs from the floor above. Sullivan had heard the first firing from the room immediately below where he was working. Realizing that something was wrong, he ran downstairs and

Winstanley went after him. As Sullivan ran along a corridor downstairs a burst of firing followed him, and he was hit in the hand. He collapsed into an opening at the bottom of the lift. It was there in that opening that the rest of the staff collected. When Winstanley came along the corridor he stood over Sullivan and pointed the gun at him.

Mrs Turley, the housekeeper, and Miss Campbell, the assistant housekeeper, ran along the passage from their room, and housemaids from upstairs came down in the lift. During the confusion Mrs Turley tried to pacify Winstanley, and Sullivan managed to get away and ran into the kitchen corridor. Winstanley said to the people standing there – all of them women: 'Don't be frightened, I wouldn't hurt any of you girls. The three of them are in there dead, Douglas, Mr Stallard, and her Ladyship.' Miss Doxford, Lady Derby's maid, and the housemaids made their way upstairs to the smoke room . . .

Another person attracted to the scene was M.

Dupuis, the chef. He tried to reason with Winstanley, and then saw Winstanley go to his room and come out wearing his mackintosh. He walked with Winstanley down one corridor into another, at the end of which was a door leading out into the grounds. In that passage M. Dupuis tried to snatch the gun from Winstanley, but received a blow on the head with the butt of it. When that blow was struck the gun went off, spraying the wall with bullets.

When the police arrived they went to the smoke-room and found Lady Derby. She had been shot and Winstanley could well be forgiven for thinking her dead. A bullet had entered the back of her neck, but had come out just below the left ear. Stallard was dead. He had five bullet wounds, two of which would certainly have killed him. Stuart also had been hit by five bullets, four of which would have killed him, in the head, chest, and abdomen .... Thirty-seven shots were fired in the house that night.

The Times, 6 NOVEMBER, 1952

Luggage van with chauffeur at Polesden Lacey, Surrey, c. 1914.
(right) 'Cabbage Castle', the castellated house designed for his guinea-pigs by Charles Lamb at Beauport House, Sussex, c. 1830.

Cabbage Castle.

The ancient residence of the Count of Valmore Cabbage — built by the Emperor Erminens I. year 40 — II — In the year 18. having become ruinous it was taken down & a very splendid edifice erected on the same site by Enceladus [illegible] Waloi —

9
Animals

Medieval castles and country houses made much use of animals. Dogs for hunting and guarding proliferated, as did hawks for hunting or horses for war, sport and transport. The animal population of a medieval complex may have exceeded its human one, even excluding the deer in the deer park or the sheep and cattle who sheltered in the outbuildings or grazed in the adjacent fields.

But they were anonymous animals, and left little permanent mark. No distinctive stable buildings survive from the period. With the exception of cats for scavenging and dogs to turn kitchen spits, they were forbidden the main house. The image of dogs rootling for bones on the rush-strewn floors of medieval halls is a fantasy invented by Walter Scott and his generation. In any well-conducted medieval or sixteenth-century hall, dogs were not allowed in.

Domestic pets may have arrived in the fifteenth century, or even earlier, but it is not until the late sixteenth and early seventeenth centuries that they begin to feature in English portraits. Their presence was dramatically illustrated at the execution of Mary, Queen of Scots, when her little dog fled for security beneath the dress of his decapitated mistress. Pets begin to appear in literature at about the same time – Lady Harington's dog, for instance. The first impressive English stables were built in the early seventeenth century. At much the same time William Cavendish, later Duke of Newcastle, was perhaps the first English landowner to make a cult of horses – to write about them and commission portraits of them, as well as building lavish stables and riding schools for them.

Even so, at Woburn in the seventeenth century, for instance, dogs are still featuring in letters and account books in a purely functional capacity. It was probably not until the eighteenth century that sporting, as opposed to lap, dogs began to be allowed into the house. Monuments to dogs and horses appeared at about the same time. Occasional menageries added an exotic note. Animal portraits abounded. Animals were becoming the companions, rather than servants, of the upper classes.

The 2nd Lord Rothschild and his team of zebras at Tring Park, Hertfordshire, c. 1900.

SIR

GERVASE

AND

THE

BEAR

1601

SIR Gervase Clifton being at a bear baiting in Nottinghamshire: when the bear broke loose and followed his son up a stairs towards a gallery where himself was, he opposed himself with his rapier against the fury of the beast, to save his son.

JOHN CHAMBERLAIN, *Letters*

DOGS

TO

BE

KEPT

OUT

OF

THE

HOUSE

1605

HE [the usher of the hall] is to see that no dogs be suffered to tarry in the hall, for they will be robbers of the alms tubs. The groom [of the hall] is to have a whip with a bell, to fear them away withall; for dogs of all kinds must be kept in their kennels and out places fit for them.

RULES FOR THE HOUSE OF AN EARL, 1605

THE

DUKE

OF

NEWCASTLE

AND

HIS

HORSES

1667

SO great a love hath my Lord for good horses! And certainly I have observed, and do verily believe, that some of them had also a particular love to my Lord; for they seemed to rejoice whensoever he came into the stables, by their trampling action, and the noise they made; nay, they would go much better in the Mannage, when my Lord was by, than when he was absent; and when he rode them himself, they seemed to take much pleasure and pride in it. But of all sorts of horses, my Lord loved Spanish horses and barbes best, saying, That Spanish horses were like princes, and barbes like gentlemen, in their kind.

DUCHESS OF NEWCASTLE, *Life of William Cavendish, Duke, Marquess and Earl of Newcastle*

Francis Russell, 4th Earl of Bedford, with his hawk and dogs. Detail from a picture attributed to Robert Peake, c. 1600.

Sir John Harrington lived at Kelston Hall in Somerset,
and this episode probably took place there.

LADY

HARINGTON'S

DOG

YOUR little dog, that barked as I came by,
I strake by hap so hard I made him cry;
And straight you put your finger in your eye,
And louring sat. I asked the reason why.
'Love me, and love my dog,' thou didst reply.
'Love as both should be loved.' – 'I will,' said I,
And sealed it with a kiss. Then by and by,
Cleared were the clouds of thy fair frowning sky.
Thus small events, great masteries may try.
For I, by this, do at their meaning guess,
That beat a whelp afore a lioness.

SIR JOHN HARINGTON, *To his wife, for striking her dog,*
Epigrams, 1618

<Big>T</Big>O the Memory
of
SIGNOR FIDO
an *Italian* of good Extraction;
who came into *England*,
not to bite us, like most of his Countrymen,
but to gain an honest livelihood.
He hunted not after Fame,
yet acquired it;
regardless of the Praise of his Friends,
but most sensible of their Love.
Tho' he lived amongst the Great,
he neither learned nor flattered any Vice.
He was no Bigot,
Though he doubted of none of the 39 Articles.
And, if to follow Nature,
and to respect the Laws of Society,
be Philosophy.
he was a perfect Philosopher;
a faithful Friend,
an agreeable companion
a loving Husband,
distinguished by a numerous Offspring,
all which he lived to see take good Courses.
In his old Age he retired
to the house of a Clergyman in the Country,
where he finished his earthly Race,
And died an Honour and an Example to the whole Species.
Reader,
This Stone is guiltless of Flattery
for he to whom it is inscribed
was not a Man
but a
GREYHOUND.

INSCRIPTION ON THE SHEPHERD'S COVE, STOWE.

(far left) A hound in front of Hutton Bonville Hall, Yorkshire. Unidentified artist, c. 1725.
(top) Lord Southampton's cat. Detail from the portrait of Henry Wriothesley, 3rd Earl of Southampton, attributed to John de Critz, 1603.
(left) 'Lord Foppington', William Beckford's dog at Fonthill Abbey, Wiltshire.

148

(top) Deer in front of Averham Park, Nottinghamshire. Detail from a picture by an unidentified artist, c. 1719.
The hunting lodge in the park of Ledston Hall, Yorkshire, with attendant cows. John Settringham, 1728.

DOGS AT CANNONS 1731

ORDERED: that all dogs whatever about the house be sent away except his Grace's be allowed to come into the parlours, and the setting dog, the mastiff bitch & kitchen garden bitch & Lord Carnarvon's little liver-coloured bitch.

HOUSEHOLD ORDERS, DUKE OF CHANDOS, 20 APRIL, 1731

MR PUREFOY'S DOGS AT SHALSTONE

1744   Dec. 30   This afternoon about 2 a clock died my pretty little bitch Chloe.

1750   May 14   Gave our Thos. Clarke for burying Killbuck, 0.0.6d.

1755   Oct. 30   To the lanes by Rawlins's house (where we lost Jewel)

Purefoy Papers

A MENAGERIE AT HORTON 1763

IN the garden or park, is a good artificial river, in which is a sloop and 2 or 3 boats; there are 2 temples, one with a portico, the other round, a triumphal arch, a Gothic bridge and a menagerie at a good distance, in which are kept a variety of wild beasts and birds: a young tiger not bigger than a cat, a bear, one monstrous large eagle, and an eagle with a white head.

REV. WILLIAM COLE, *Account of Tour with Horace Walpole*

Horses in an unidentified country-house stable, c. 1740.

A MENAGERIE AT HARDWICK C. 1800

THE late Duke used to dine here, as he supp'd at Brooks's, with his hat on, which his friends gave as the reason for his being so fond of Hardwick. His son turned the recess where the billiard table now stands into a kind of menagerie: a fishing net nailed up under the curtain confined the rabbits, hedgehogs, squirrels, guinea pigs, and white mice, that were the joy of his life from 8 to 12 years old, the smell caused by these quadrupeds was overpowering . . . but he would have been very much surprised had any objection been made to their residence here. A tree stood in the middle for the unhappy birds – caught by John Hall the gamekeeper – to perch on, and an owl made its melancholy hooting in one of the corners.

6TH DUKE OF DEVONSHIRE, *Handbook*

FAITHFUL DOGS AT FONTHILL 1812

THE poor animals Caroline and Spotty, recognising the carriage from a distance, shot towards me like arrows and, jumping on my lap, showed their genuine delight by innumerable barks and licks. They're lovelier and more attractive than ever, and I adore them – a hundred times more than the other limited, chilly, touchy members of my family. Goodbye, goodbye, I'm going out for a walk with them . . .

WILLIAM BECKFORD

150
Pugs at Wilton House, Wiltshire, in the 1860s. Gladys Herbert in the background.
(right) A formal garden, engraved on the frontispiece of *Catalogus Plantarum . . .*, published by the Society of Gardeners, 1730.

10
Parks
&
Gardens

*T*he image of abundance is one of the most powerful of those connected with country houses: abundance flowing into the houses, for the benefit of the families who lived in them and their guests, and out of them to the families living on their estates; abundance derived from woods, fields, lakes, and rivers; and above all abundance of flowers, fruits and vegetables in and from country-house orchards and gardens.

Ben Jonson celebrated the abundance of fruit at Penshurst; and the letters of Lady de l'Isle, mistress of Penshurst in Jonson's time, are full of references to fruit being sent up from its orchards to her husband in London or at court. A sense of abundance impregnates descriptions of sixteenth- and seventeenth-century gardens, and the numerous bird's-eye views of country houses which were painted in the first half of the eighteenth century.

This abundance seemed like a recreation of Paradise to contemporaries. But it existed in a framework of formal paths, clipped trees, statues and artificial grottoes. In the course of the eighteenth century another image of Paradise, equally powerful in its own way, largely replaced the old one. This was a paradise of Arcadian seclusion, of what appeared to be untouched nature, of magical demesnes hidden from the outside world by walls or encircling belts of trees and enclosing great Palladian mansions at their heart. Within the walls was open grassland dotted with clumps of noble trees, sweeping lakes reflecting the sky, or tree-lined glades in which herds of deer freely roamed and grazed in the shadow of classical temples. The image was a seductive one, but it did not seduce everyone. There were those, like the painter Constable, who distrusted it because its effect was to cut houses off from the real country and the real world.

Flower gardens came back into favour in the nineteenth century. A new phenomenon appeared; the owner-gardeners, emerging with baskets and secateurs to weed, cut and plant in the gardens themselves. This was the world of Gertrude Jekyll. She designed for many country houses, although she did not own one herself. I cannot resist quoting her remarks about the comments of visitors to gardens; they will strike a sympathetic chord in many country-house gardeners of today.

152

View from the north partico at Stowe House, Buckinghamshire (detail). Engraved after Jacques Rigaud, 1739.

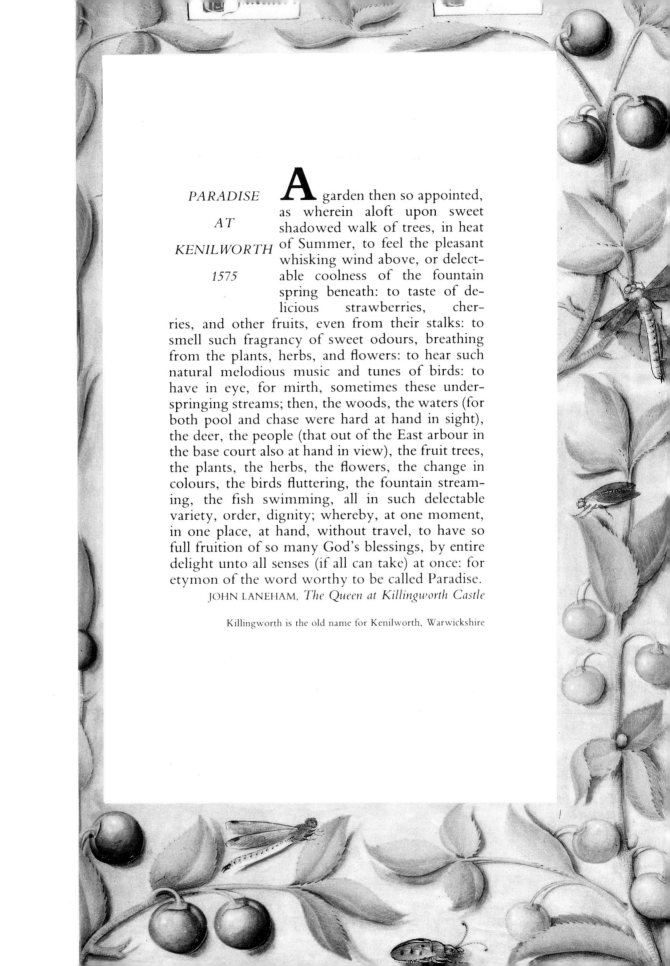

PARADISE AT KENILWORTH 1575

A garden then so appointed, as wherein aloft upon sweet shadowed walk of trees, in heat of Summer, to feel the pleasant whisking wind above, or delectable coolness of the fountain spring beneath: to taste of delicious strawberries, cherries, and other fruits, even from their stalks: to smell such fragrancy of sweet odours, breathing from the plants, herbs, and flowers: to hear such natural melodious music and tunes of birds: to have in eye, for mirth, sometimes these under-springing streams; then, the woods, the waters (for both pool and chase were hard at hand in sight), the deer, the people (that out of the East arbour in the base court also at hand in view), the fruit trees, the plants, the herbs, the flowers, the change in colours, the birds fluttering, the fountain streaming, the fish swimming, all in such delectable variety, order, dignity; whereby, at one moment, in one place, at hand, without travel, to have so full fruition of so many God's blessings, by entire delight unto all senses (if all can take) at once: for etymon of the word worthy to be called Paradise.

JOHN LANEHAM, *The Queen at Killingworth Castle*

Killingworth is the old name for Kenilworth, Warwickshire

RICHARD

CAREW

CELEBRATES

HIS

FISH

POND

AT

ANTONY

AND

HIS

PLANS

FOR

IT

1610

I wait not at the lawyer's gates,
Nor shoulder climbers down the stairs;
I vaunt not manhood by debates,
I envy not the miser's fears;
    But mean in state, and calm in sprite,
    My fishful pond is my delight.
There sucking mullet, swallowing bass,
Side-walking crab, wry-mouthed fluke,
And slip-fist eel, as evenings pass,
For safe bait at due place do look,
    Bold to approach, quick to espy,
    Greedy to catch, ready to fly.

I carried once a purpose to build a little wooden banqueting house on the island in my pond, which because some other may (perhaps) elsewhere put in execution, it will not do much amiss to deliver you the plot as the same was devised for me by that perfectly accomplished gentleman, the late Sir Arthur Champernowne.

The island is square, with four rounds at the corners, like Mount Edgecumbe. This should first have been planched over, and railed about with balusters. In the midst there should have risen a boarded room of the like fashion but lesser proportion, so to leave sufficient space between that and the rails for a walk round about. This square room should withinside have been ceiled round-wise, and in three of the places where the round joined with the square, as many windows should have been set; the fourth should have served for a door. Of the four turrets shut out by this round, one should have made a kitchen, the second a storehouse to keep the fishing implements, the third a buttery, and the fourth a stair for ascending to the next loft; which next loft should have risen on the flat roof of the lower, in a round form, but of a lesser size again, so to leave a second terrace like the other. And as the square room below was ceiled round, so should this upper round room be ceiled square, to the end that where the side walls and ceiling joined, three windows and a door might likewise find their places. The void spaces between the round and square he would have turned to cupboards and boxes, for keeping other necessary utensils towards these fishing feasts.

RICHARD CAREW, *The Survey of Cornwall*

(Left, and elsewhere at borders). John Evelyn's garden tools, from his unfinished and unpublished *Elysium Britannicum*.

William Lawson may have served as gardener to Sir Henry Bellasis, of Newburgh Priory, Yorkshire, to whom his book is dedicated.

THE

DELIGHTS

OF

AN

ORCHARD

1618

WHAT can your eye desire to see, your ears to hear, your mouth to take, or your nose to smell, that is not to be had in an Orchard, with abundance of variety? What more delightsome than an infinite variety of sweet smelling flowers decking with sundry colours, the green mantle of the earth, the universal mother of us all, so by them despotted, so dyed, that all the World cannot sample them, and wherein it is more fit to admire the Dyer, than imitate his Workmanship, colouring not only the earth, but decking the air, and sweetening every breath and spirit.

The Rose red, Damask, Velvet, and double double Province-Rose, the sweet Musk-Rose double and single, the double and single white-Rose: The fair and sweet-scenting Woodbine, double and single, and double double. Purple Cowslips, and double Cowslips, and double double Cowslips, Primrose double and single. The Violet nothing behind the best, for smelling sweetly. A thousand more will provoke your content.

And all these by the skill of your Gardener, so comelily and orderly placed in your borders and squares, and so intermingled, that one looking thereon, cannot but wonder to see, what Nature, corrected by Art, can do.

When you behold in divers corners of your Orchard *Mounts* of stone or wood, curiously wrought within and without, or of earth covered with Fruit-trees, Kentish Cherries, Damsons, Plums, &c. with stairs of precious workmanship; and in some corner (or more) a true Dial or Clock, and some Antick works; and especially silver-sounding Music, mixed Instruments, and Voices, gracing all the rest: How will you be rapt with Delight?

Large Walks, broad and long, close and open, like the *Tempegroves* in *Thessaly*, raised with gravel and sand, having seats and banks of Camomile; all this delights the mind, and brings health to the body.

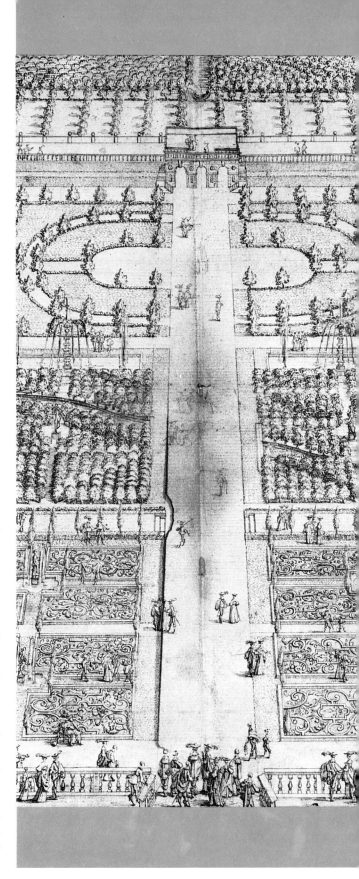

155

Design for the garden at Wilton House, Wiltshire, by Isaac de Caus, late 1630s (detail).

View now with delight the works of your own hands, your Fruit-trees of all sorts, loaden with sweet blossoms, and fruit of all tastes, operations, and colours: your trees standing in comely order, which way soever you look.

Your border on every side hanging and dropping with Feberries, Raspberries, Barberries, Currants, and the Roots of your trees powdered with Strawberries, Red, White, and Green, what a pleasure is this! Your Gardener can frame your lesser wood to the shape of men armed in the field, ready to give battle; of swift-running Greyhounds, or of well-scented and true-running Hounds to chase the Deer, or hunt the Hare. This kind of hunting shall not waste your Corn, nor much your Coin.

Mazes well framed a man's height, may perhaps make your friend wander in gathering of Berries till he cannot recover himself without your help.

To have occasion to exercise within your Orchard, it shall be a pleasure to have a bowling-Alley, or rather (which is more manly, and more healthful) a pair of Butts, to stretch your Arms.

Rosemary and sweet Eglantine are seemly Ornaments about a Door or Window, and so is Woodbine . . .

And in mine own opinion, I could highly commend your Orchard, if either through it, or hard by it, there should run a pleasant River with silver streams, you might sit in your Mount, and angle a peckled Trout, sleighty Eel, or some other dainty Fish. Or Moats, whereon you may row with a Boat, and fish with Nets.

Stores of Bees in a warm and dry Bee-house, comely made of Firboards, to sing, and sit, and feed upon your flowers and sprouts, make a pleasant noise and sight. For cleanly and innocent Bees, of all other things, love, and become, and thrive in an Orchard . . .

WILLIAM LAWSON, *A New Orchard and Garden*

156

(right) The garden at Denham Place, Buckinghamshire. Detail from a painting of c. 1705 by an unidentified artist.

LORD

AND

LADY

FAIRFAX

TAKE

A

MORNING

WALK

WITH

THEIR

DAUGHTER

1651

WHEN in the east the morning ray
Hangs out the colours of the day
The bee through these known alleys hums,
Beating the dian with its drums.
Then flowers their drowsy eyelids raise,
Their silken ensigns each displays,
And dries its pan yet dank with dew,
And fills its flask with odours new.

These, as their governor goes by,
In fragrants volleys they let fly;
And to salute their governess
Again as great a charge they press:
None for the virgin nymph; for she
Seems with the flowers a flower to be.
And think so still! though not compare
With breath so sweet, or cheek so fair.

Well shot ye firemen! Oh how sweet
And round your equal fires do meet;
Whose shrill report no ear can tell,
But echoes to the eye and smell.
See how the flowers, as at parade,
Under their colours stand displayed:
Each regiment in order grows,
That of the tulip, pink and rose.
But when the vigilant patrol
Of stars walk round about the pole,
Their leaves, that to the stalks are curled,
Seem to their staves the ensigns furled.
Then in some flower's beloved hut
Each bee as sentinel is shut;
And sleeps so too: but if once stirred
She runs you through, nor asks the word.

FROM ANDREW MARVELL, *Upon Appleton House*

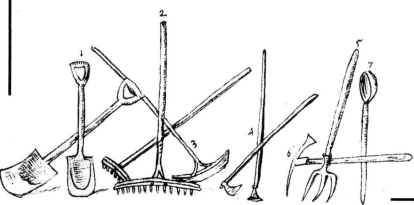

THOMAS

BUSHELL'S

GROTTO

AT

ENSTONE

1667

AFTER his master the lord chancellor died, he married and lived at Enston, Oxon; where having some land lying on the hanging of a hill facing the south, at the foot whereof runs a fine clear stream which petrifies, and where is a pleasant solitude, he spoke to his servant Jack Sydenham to get a labourer to clear some boscage which grew on the side of the hill, and also to dig a cavity in the hill to sit, and read or contemplate ... The workman had not worked an hour before he discovers not only a rock, but a rock of an unusual figure with pendants like icicles as at Wookey Hole, which was the occasion of making that delicate grotto and those fine walks.

Here in fine weather he would walk all night. Jack Sydenham sang rarely: so did his other servant, Mr Batty. They went very gent. in clothes, and he loved them as his children.

In the time of the civil wars his hermitage over the rocks at Enston were hung with black-bayes; ... When the queen-mother came to Oxon to the king, she either brought (as I think) or somebody gave her an entire mummy from Egypt, a great rarity, which her majesty gave to Mr Bushell, but I believe long before this time the dampness of the place has spoiled it with mouldiness. The grotto below looks just south; so that when it artificially

Fountain in a Formal Garden, from Stephen Switzer *An Introduction to Hydrostaticks and Hydraulics*, 1729.

rains, upon the turning of a cock, you are entertained with a rainbow. In a very little pond (no bigger than a basin) opposite to the rock, and hard by, stood a Neptune, neatly cut in wood, holding his trident in his hand, and aiming with it at a duck which perpetually turned round with him, and a spaniel swimming after her.

JOHN AUBREY, *Brief Lives*

The grotto at Enstone, from Plot's *Natural History of Oxfordshire*, 1677.

Col. Pl. XVI A Gothick
Pavilion at Painswick
House, Gloucestershire.
Thomas Robbins,
c.1760.

DELIGHTS

OF

A

GROTTO

1677

THEREFORE either in the side of some decline of a Hill, or under some Mount or Terrace artificially raised, may you make a place of repose, cool and fresh in the greatest heats. It may be arched over with stone or brick and you may give it what light or entrance you please. You may make secret rooms and passages within it, and in the outer room may you have all those before-mentioned water-works, for your own or your friends' divertisements. It is a place capable of giving you so much pleasure and delight, that you may bestow not undeserved'ly what cost you please on it, by paving it with marble or immuring it with stone or rock-work, either natural or artificially resembling the excellencies of nature.

JOHN WOOLRIDGE, *Systema Horticultura*

EVELYN

INSTRUCTS

THE

PUBLIC

1664

MARCH. Now you may set your oranges, lemons, myrtles, oleanders, *lentisci*, dates, aloes, amomums, and like tender trees and plants on the portico, or with the windows and doors of the greenhouses and conservatories open, for eight or ten days before April, or earlier, if the season invite (that is, if the sharp winds be past) to acquaint them gradually with the air; I say gradually and carefully; for this change is the most critical of the whole year; trust not therefore the nights too confidently, unless the weather be thoroughly settled.

JOHN EVELYN, *Kalendarium Hortense*

EVELYN

INSTRUCTS

HIS

GARDENER

1687

EVERY fortnight look on Saturday to your seed and root boxes, to air & preserve them from mouldiness & vermin. Look every month (the last day of it) & see in what state the Beehives are: and every day, about noon if the weather be warm, and the Bees hang out for swarms; having your hives prepared & ready dressed.

The Tools are to be carried into the Toolhouse, and all other instruments set in their places, every night when you leave work: & in wet weather you are to cleanse, sharpen, & repair them.

The heaps of Dung, & Magazines of Mould &c: are to be stirred once every quarter, the first week.

In April, Mid-August, clip Cypress, Box, & generally most evergreen hedges: & closes, as quick-sets.

Prune standard-fruit & Mural Trees the later end of July, & beginning of August for the second spring: Vines in January & exuberant branches that hinder the fruit ripening in June.

The Gardener is every night to ask what Roots, salading, garnishing, &c will be used the next day, which he is accordingly to bring to the Cook in the morning; and therefore from time to time inform her what garden provision & fruit is ripe and in season to be spent.

He is also to Gather, & bring in to the House-Keeper all such Fruit of Apples, pears, quinces, Cherries, Grapes, peaches, Apricots, Mulberries, strawberry, Raspberries, Corinths, Cornelians, Nuts, Plums, & generally all sort of Fruit, as the season ripens them, gathering all the windfalls by themselves: That they may be immediately spent, or reserved in the Fruit & store-house.

He may not dispose of any the above said Fruit nor sell any Artichoke, Cabbages, Asparagus, Melons, strawberries, Raspberries, Wall, or standard & dwarf fruit, Roses, Violets, Cloves, or any Greens, or other flowers or plants, without first asking, and having leave of his Master or Mistress; nor till there be sufficient of all garden furniture for the Grounds stock and families use.

JOHN EVELYN, *Directions for the Gardiner at Sayes Court*

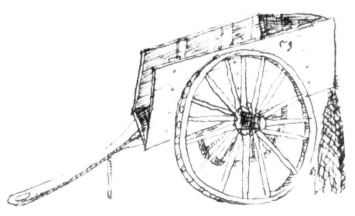

Col. Pl. XVII (left) Garden bridge at Chiswick House, Middlesex. Detail from the picture by P.A. Rysbrack, c.1729–30.

GARDEN GEAR AT HOLKHAM, 1761

In the Pleasure Grounds and Orangery

20	Barrow Chairs	20	Small Winsor Chairs
3	Double Seated Chairs	6	Compass Back Chairs

Plants and Trees in Tubs and Pots

250	Pines in Pots [pineapples]	25	Double and Single Leafed Myrtles in Pots
4	Citrons in Tubs		
46	Orange Trees in Tubs	70	Seedling Oranges in Pots
9	Lemon Trees in Pots	13	Aloes in Pots
3	Broad Leafed Myrtles in Tubs		

Working Tools and Utensils

11	Scythes	1	Pair of Garden Shears
6	Rakes	1	Mallet and Pruning Chisel
5	Dutch Hoes	2	Mattocks
8	English Hoes	1	Flag Shovel
8	Forks	1	Edging Tool
3	Jets	2	Pair of Iron Reels with Lines
6	Watering Pots		
2	Tin Pipes for Watering Pines	2	Hand Saws
		1	Grindstone and Frame
1	House Engine	4	Rubstones
1	Brass Hand Engine	1	Cucumber cutter
2	Wooden Hand Engines [all for water]	91	Frames Glazed for Melons Pines and Cucumbers
3	Leather Pipes	35	Frames for the Fire Walls
1	Suction Pipe	21	Hand Glasses
1	Brass Pipe	9	Bell Glasses
1	Rose [for sprinkling]		Netting in five Parcels
2	Thermometers		A Number of Old Mats
2	Shovels	8	Common Wheel Barrows
4	Hammers	2	Water Barrows
1	Hook [Sickle]	3	Water Tubs
1	Hatchet	3	Stone Rollers
2	Iron Rollers	1	Large Fruit Basket
5	Boots for Horses to Roll the Garden with	8	Bushell Baskets
		3	Water Pails
8	Hand Baskets for Fruit		

INVENTORY, *Holkham MSS*

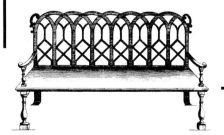
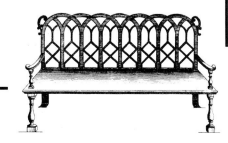

A gentleman's park is what I abhor. It is not beauty because it is not nature.

JOHN CONSTABLE

(left) Design for a garden seat. Charles Over, 1758.
(above) Captain Cook's monument and the Grenville Column, in the gardens of Stowe House, Buckinghamshire. J.C. Nattes, 1805.

View of the park from the terrace of Woburn Abbey, Bedfordshire, as proposed by Humphrey Repton.

YOU might draw, but I can't describe, the enchanting scenes of the park; it is a hill of three miles, but broke into all manner of beauty; such lawns, such woods, rills, cascades, and a thickness of verdure quite to the summit of the hill, and commanding such a vale of towns, and meadows, and woods extending quite to the Black Mountain in Wales, that I quite forgot my favourite Thames! Indeed, I prefer nothing to Hagley but Mount Edgecombe. There is extreme taste in the park: the seats are not the best, but there is not one absurdity. There is a ruined castle, built by Miller, that would get him his freedom even of Strawberry: it has the true rust of the Baron's Wars. Then there is a scene of a small lake, with cascades falling down such a Parnassus! with a circular temple on the distant eminence; and there is such a fairy dale, with more cascades gushing out of the rocks! and there is a hermitage, so exactly like those in Sadeler's prints, on the brow of a shady mountain, stealing peeps into the glorious world below! and there is such a pretty well under a wood, like the Samaritan woman's in a picture of Nicolo Poussin! and there is such a wood without the park, enjoying such a prospect! and there is such a mountain on t'other side of the park commanding such a prospect, that I wore out my eyes with gazing, my feet with climbing, and my tongue and my vocabulary with commending.

WALPOLE TO RICHARD BENTLEY, SEPTEMBER, 1753

IN England, when a new manner is universally adopted, in which no appearance of art is tolerated, our gardens differ very little from common fields, so closely is common nature copied in most of them ... and a stranger is often at a loss to know whether he is walking in a meadow, or in a pleasure ground, made and kept at very considerable expense. He sees nothing to amuse him, nothing to

excite his curiosity, nor any thing to keep up his attention.

At his first entrance, he is treated with the sight of a large green field, scattered over with a fair straggling trees, and verged with a confused border of little shrubs and flowers; upon further inspection, he finds a little serpentine path, turning in regular 'esses' amongst the shrubs of the border, upon which he is to go round, to look on one side at what he has already seen, the large green field ... From time to time he perceives a little seat or temple stuck up against a wall; he rejoices at the discovery, sits down, rests his wearied limbs, and then reels on again, cursing the line of beauty, till spent with fatigue, half roasted by the sun, for there is never any shade, and tired for want of entertainment, he resolves to see no more.

Vain resolution! there is but one path; he must either drag on to the end, or return back by the tedious way he came.

WILLIAM CHAMBERS, *Dissertation on Oriental Gardening*

THE KITCHEN-GARDEN AT TRENTHAM 1828

THEY were out when we came. I rushed to the *potager* – you know my weakness – and walked up and down between spinach and dahlias in ecstasy. This is in many ways a beautiful place and the *tenue*, the neatness, the training of flowers and fruit trees, gates, enclosures, hedges, are what in no other country is dreamt of; and then there is a repose, a *laisser aller*, a freedom, and a security in a *vie de château* that no other destiny offers one. I feel when I set out to

165

In the garden at Sedgwick Park, Sussex, 1901.

walk as if alone in the world – nothing but trees and birds; but then comes the enormous satisfaction of always finding a man dressing a hedge, or a woman in a gingham and a black bonnet on her knees picking up weeds, the natural gendarmerie of the country, and the most comfortable well-organized country.

HARRIET, COUNTESS GRANVILLE, TO HER SISTER, LADY CARLISLE, 1828

THE
DUCHESS
OF
EDINBURGH
IS
BORED
AT
EASTWELL
PARK
1884

YOU seem to enjoy your country life. I could also enjoy it under different circumstances though I find that inland English country seats are so exactly alike that I never find anything new in them to describe or admire: the same turf, the same lawns and trees, the everlasting evergreens, so charming in the South and so depressing during an English winter, the same endless parks with their elms and beeches and their meagre deer and idiotic sheep and lambs which get so dreadfully on my nerves just now with their bleating. Ravens and blackbirds, as stately and prim as the rest of the depressing scenery, picking up worms, and stiff beds of flowers in the so called pleasure grounds. No high waving grass with thousands of flowers, no real forests with valleys and streams, no gaily dressed peasants men and women returning from their field work and singing merrily, like one sees abroad.

THE DUCHESS OF EDINBURGH TO A FRIEND, EASTWELL PARK, KENT, APRIL, 1884.

MISS
JEKYLL
SPEAKS
HER
MIND
1899

IT is a curious thing that many people, even amongst those who profess to know something about gardening, when I show them something successful – the crowning reward of much care and labour – refuse to believe that any pains have been taken about it. They will ascribe it to chance, to the goodness of my soil, and even more commonly to some supposed occult influence of my own – to anything rather

than the plain fact that I love it well enough to give it plenty of care and labour. They assume a tone of complimentary banter, kindly meant no doubt, but to me rather distasteful, to this effect: 'Oh, yes, of course, it will grow with you; anything will grow for you; you have only to look at a thing and it will grow.' I have to pump up a laboured smile and accept the remark with what grace I can, as a necessary civility to the stranger within my gates, but it seems to me evident that those who say things do not understand the love of a garden.

GERTRUDE JEKYLL, *Wood and Garden*

SUCCESS
AT
SISSINGHURST
1937

NEVER has Sissinghurst looked more lovely or been more appreciated. I must say, Farley has made the place look like a gentleman's garden, and you with your extraordinary taste have made it look like nobody's garden but your own. I think the secret of your gardening is simply that you have the courage to abolish ugly or unsuccessful flowers. Except for those beastly red-hot pokers which you have a weakness for, there is not an ugly flower in the whole place. Then I think, *si j'ose m'exprimer ainsi*, that the design is really rather good. I mean we have got what we wanted to get – a perfect proportion between the classic and the romantic, between the element of expectation and the element of surprise. Thus the main axes are terminated in a way to satisfy expectation, yet they are in themselves so tricky that they also cause surprise. But the point of the garden will not be apparent until the hedges have grown up, especially (most important of all) the holly hedge in the flower garden. But it is lovely, lovely, lovely – and you must be pleased with your work.

HAROLD NICOLSON TO VITA SACKVILLE-WEST, JUNE 1937

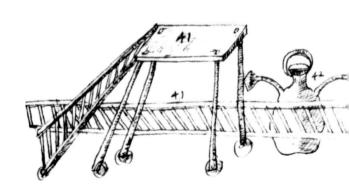

166

(right) Designs for water-closet at Felbrigg Hall, Norfolk. Robert Brettingham, 1794.

11
Plumbing,
Or
The
Lack
Of
It

*O*n the whole, the history of plumbing, and of technology generally in English country houses, has been one of installing gadgets which fail to work. It is a two-steps-forward one-step-back story. In medieval houses the privy or garderobe system was introduced as the great new hope for salubrious living. It was a system of shafts, dropping into pits, drains, or moats. But the walls of the shafts grew filthy, and drains, moats and houses stank after they had been occupied for a few weeks. In the sixteenth century there was a reaction in favour of the close-stool – a box containing a receptacle, which a servant could remove and empty at a convenient distance from the house.

In the late seventeenth century water-closets and plunge baths enjoyed a vogue among the very rich. But before the invention of the S-bend trap, water closets smelt. Earth closets came into favour in their places.

In the late eighteenth century water closets at last broke the technological barrier. At the same period, or a few decades later, tub baths and radiators appeared, along with hot water to service them. Unfortunately, the water was seldom hot. Open fires, and hip baths filled by servants carrying water in cans, were as effective, if not more so. All foreign visitors commented on the cold of English houses. Bathrooms did not really establish themselves adequately until the 1920s – and then only in some houses.

In the 1950s oil-fired central heating became the new toy of country-house owners. A picture or a few pieces of silver were sold to pay for its installation, and the boiler was shown to visitors with as much pride as a prize hunter. Then oil prices soared, and cold descended on the houses once again.

GLEDHOW HALL. LEEDS.
J. Kitson Junr Esqr
BATH-ROOM IN BURMANTOFT FAIENCE.

168

A bathroom in Burmantoft faience, installed at Gledhow Hall, near Leeds, c. 1885.

A

SERVANT

EXHORTED

C. 1460

SEE the privy house for easement be fair, sweet and clean
And that the boards thereupon be covered with cloth fair and green,
And the hole himself, look there no board be seen.
Thereon a fair cushion, the ordure no man to demean.
Look there be blanket, cotton, or linen to wipe the nether end
And ever when he calleth, wait ready and attend
With basin and ewer, and on your shoulder a towel, my friend.

JOHN RUSSELL, *Book of Nurture*

BESS

OF

HARDWICK'S

CLOSE

STOOL

1601

IN a little room within my Lady's Chamber: a Close stool covered with blue cloth stitched with white, with red and black silk fringe . . .

HARDWICK
INVENTORY

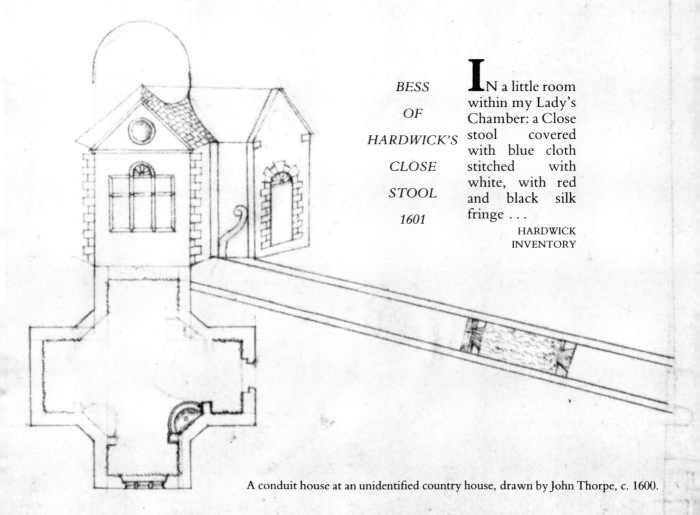

A conduit house at an unidentified country house, drawn by John Thorpe, c. 1600.

A

BATH

FOR

THE

DEVON-

SHIRES:

CHATSWORTH

1697

THERE is a fine grotto, all stone pavement, roof and sides. This is designed to supply all the house with water besides several fancies to make diversion. Within this is a bathing room, the walls all with blue and white marble, the pavement mixed one stone white, another black, another of the red rance marble; the bath is one entire marble all white finely veined with blue and is made smooth, but had it been as finely polished as some, it would have been the finest marble that could be seen; it was as deep as one's middle on the outside and you went down steps into the bath big enough for two people; at the upper end are two cocks to let in one hot the other cold water, to attemper it as persons please; the windows are all private glass.

CELIA FIENNES, *Journeys*

DANGERS

OF

A

TOOTHBRUSH

1721

I must now mention a thing of an inferior kind, which perhaps my Love will not easily admit of, though I am fully satisfied of the truth of it . . .; which is, that using a brush to yr teeth and gums (as you constantly do) will certainly prove in time extreme-ly injurious to them both, and especially to the last, which will be quite worn away by it; and I beg of ye for the future to use a sponge in its room.

SIR JOHN PHILIPPS, OF PICTON CASTLE, PEMBROKESHIRE, TO LADY PHILIPPS, 7 NOVEMBER, 1721

The plunge-bath at Stowe House, Buckinghamshire. J.C. Nattes, 1807.

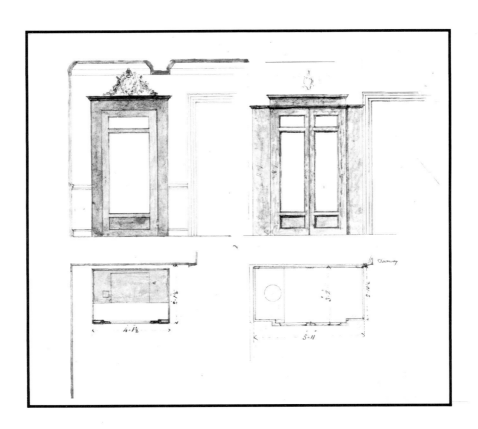

DUCAL WATER-CLOSETS AT CANNONS 1725

BETWEEN cabinet and his Grace's dressing room.
Marble pavement, marble lining and marble basin.
Japanned seat, fretwork ceiling with gilding, painting
by Scarptena

£251.29

In passage outside library leading to waiting room.
Marble basin to the water closet, plug, cock and handles

£12

Next her Grace's closet
Marble paving and skirting and marble basin.
Dutch tiles, wainscot seat, wainscot bath lined with
red, Japanned close stool, curtains.

£78:4:0

CANNONS INVENTORY

171

Designs for ducal water-closets to be concealed in cupboards at Stowe.

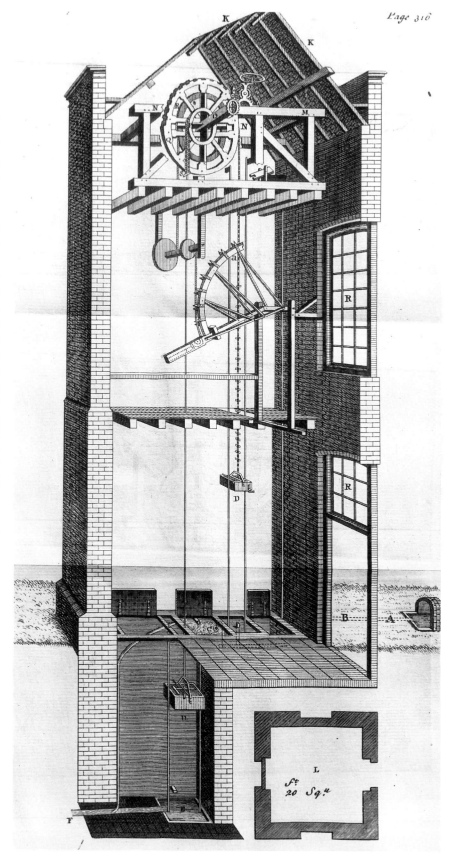

I think it the best place imaginable. Should not the inside be stuccoed, or how do you do it? how many holes? There must be one for a child; and I would have it as light as possible. There must be a good broad place to set a candle on, and a place to keep paper. I think the holes should be wide and rather oblong, and the seats broad and not quite level, and rather low before, but rising behind. Tho' the better the plainer, it should be neat.

WILLIAM WYNDHAM TO ROBERT
FRIARY, 1751

'Mr Gerves's Multiplying Wheel Bucket Engine', installed to supply water to Chicheley House, Buckinghamshire, c. 1729.

EVERY big country house boasted one or more large iron tanks encased in mahogany, evidently designed to do duty as baths and – judging from their size – designed to accommodate several people at once. At one end of these tanks was a brass dial on which were inscribed the words 'hot', 'cold' and 'waste', and a revolving handle manoeuvred an indicator into position opposite such of these inscriptions as a prospective bather might be attracted to ... A call on the hot water supply, however, did not meet with an effusive or even a warm response. A succession of sepulchral rumblings was succeeded by the appearance of a small geyser of rust-coloured water, heavily charged with dead earwigs and bluebottles. This continued for a couple of minutes or so and then entirely ceased. The only perceptible difference between the hot water and the cold lay in its colour and in the cargo of defunct life which the former bore on its bosom. Both were stone cold.

In the face of such uninviting conditions, it can readily be understood that these huge enamelled iron tanks were not popular as instruments of cleanliness. In fact, although Eastwell and Baron's Court, two big country houses in which much of my early youth was passed, each boasted two of such baths, I have never heard of any of the four being used for the purpose for which they were no doubt originally designed. As boys, my brother and I found the lower bath at Eastwell admirably suited to the trial trips of our toy boats; and at Barons Court, where we had no toy boats, it was our practice to use the ground floor bath as an occasional aquarium.

LORD ERNEST HAMILTON, *Old Days and New*

IF there be a bathroom in an English house, it must answer for the whole household. If there be a lift, it stops at the dining-room floor, although coals and water have to be carried to the higher stories. If hot and cold water be laid on, it is only in certain select apartments. Ventilators are almost unknown, except, perhaps, that antiquated sort which are let into the windows. Heated air is considered unhealthy, and so the ladies and children sit before the grate-fires with shawls over their shoulders, and catch cold in order to prevent injuring their lungs. Gas is making its way into all English houses now, but is still forbidden to be used in sleeping apartments, although the smoke from even a wax candle is hardly preferable to the odour of the small amount of gas which can possibly escape. No stranger can live for a week in an English house and not be ill from exposure to the chilly halls and stairways, even if he succeed in making himself comfortable before the fire. The English wrap themselves up to cross the hall as though they were going out of doors. Refrigerators are comparatively a new invention here. Iced water is vetoed as injurious to the teeth. It is true that in England one generally has no trouble to keep cool; the trouble is ever to get warm.

STEPHEN FISKE, *American Photographs*

A BATH FOR MR LEES-MILNE THONOCK HALL LINCS 1947

PITCH dark when called by a dear old man who entered my bedroom and pulled back the heavy curtains. Rats' tails of grey fog swirled across the window panes. Tenderly this old retainer brought into the room a red blanket which he spread before the empty fire grate. Then he trundled a small tin hip-bath on to the red blanket. Then he brought a brass can of tepid water, enough to cover the bottom of the bath. The room must have been several degrees below zero. He might have been a ghost performing the customary function of a hundred years ago. But one hundred years ago there would have been a blazing fire in the grate.

JAMES LEES-MILNE, *Caves of Ice*

(right) Detail from the monument to Sir William and Lady Catherine Savage. Elmley Castle, Worcestershire, c. 1616.

12
Birth
&
Death

Many of the most dramatic or poignant incidents in country houses were connected with births or deaths, as at all levels of society. But they had an additional significance there, because of the worldly stakes involved. They ensured the continuance of a line or marked the transfer of property and the beginning of a new reign. They called for celebration. Christening parties tended to be of a relatively minor nature, however, perhaps because death in childhood was so common that it seemed to be tempting providence to make too much of a show. With a funeral one knew exactly where one was.

Country-house funerals could be formidable affairs. A public state funeral is the closest equivalent today. They were often preceded by the lying-in-state of the corpse, for the benefit of neighbours and tenantry who filed past by the hundred. The whole house could be shrouded in black, and hundreds of black-robed mourners formed a great

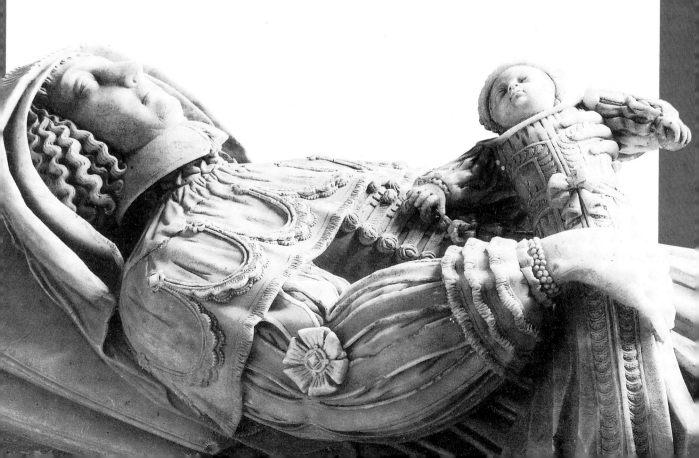

funeral cortege from the house to the church. After the coffin had been lowered into the grave, or carried into the vault, the upper servants symbolically broke their staffs of office, and threw them after the coffin. Then came the funeral feast, at which up to a thousand people could gorge and get drunk in and around the house. The central feast took place in the great chamber, and was presided over by the chief mourner sitting under a black canopy.

The lavishness at funerals was generally on the decrease in the eighteenth and nineteenth centuries, although it survived at some great houses, as the description of the funeral of the Duchess of Rutland in 1825 makes clear.

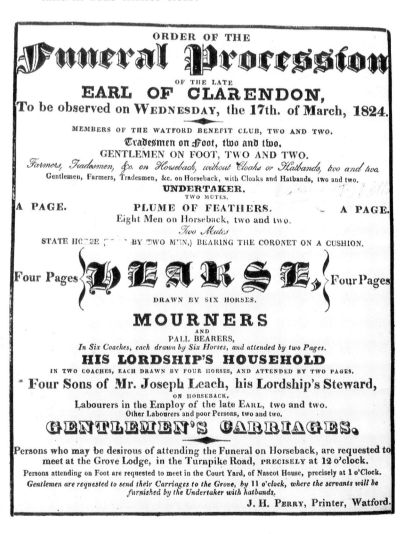

Order of the Funeral Procession of the Earl of Clarendon, 1824.
Col. Pl. XVIII (right) The christening of the child of Sir Henry and Lady Unton, c.1596.

WHICWOD

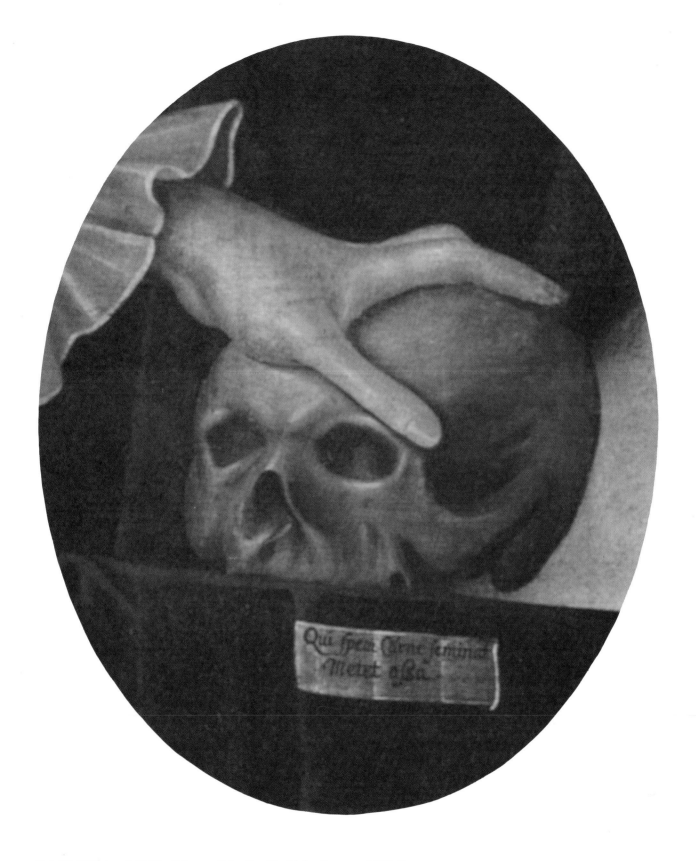

Col. Pl. XIX (top left) The Saltonstall family. David des Granges, 1636–7.

Col. Pl. XX (left) The Cholmondeley Sisters. Unidentified artist, c.1600.

Col. Pl. XXI Detail from the portrait of Sir Thomas Aston at the death-bed of his wife. John Souch, 1635.

Col. Pls. XXII and XXIII. Two portraits of babies by Joshua Reynolds: (top) Georgiana, Duchess of Devonshire, and her daughter Georgiana, later Countess of Carlisle, c.1784; (above) Caroline, Duchess of Marlborough, with her daughter, also Caroline, who became Viscountess Clifden, c.1764–5.

Food eaten at the funeral feast of Lady Katherine Howard, Framlingham Castle, 1465

MOURNING

FOR

LADY

KATHERINE

1465

2	great boars	48	partridges
12	great oxen	14	pheasants
40	sheep	7	peacocks
12	hogs	36	mallards
70	pigs	36	plovers
12	swans	800	eggs
80	geese	30	gal. milk
200	conyes [rabbits]	3	gal. honey
24	capons	32	barrels beer
140	chickens	3	pipes wine
30	ducks		

PASTON LETTERS

HOW

WILLIAM

WENTWORTH

GOT

HIS

BIRTH-

MARK

C. 1550

SIR William Gascoigne coming to hunt the buck in the park at Wentworth Woodhouse before my said father was born (as he told me) the buck at last was taken in the pond near the house by the hounds. Wherefore my father's mother, being then great with child of him, came with her mother in law to bid him welcome &c. Whereupon he, being of a wild wilful disposition, looked in my grand mother's face (for in truth I have heard discreet men say that he had a strange gift to conjecture beforehand many things that were to come) and swore a great oath that she was with child with a boy and earnestly swore he would with the tip of his finger only, dipped in the buck's blood, mark that boy for his own upon his mother's cheek; saying he was assured that it would be a boy and having a beard the red spot would not be seen, when he was a man. She refusing, he threatened to lay all his whole bloody hands upon her face, unless &c. Thereupon my grandmother, seeing no remedy, suffered him to touch her cheek with the tip of his finger dipped in blood, which mark, said my father to me, I here show unto thee. And opening the hairs of his beard, I there saw it plainly.

SIR WILLIAMS'S ACCOUNT OF THE PROVIDENCES
VOUCHSAFED HIS FAMILY, WRITTEN 1607

Extracts from the will of Dame Margaret Verney, of Claydon, 2 May, 1639, addressed to her son Ralph.

Give to your wife my diamond clasps, sheep head, and the rest of my odd diamonds and my sable muff and six of my new great smocks. If cook is with me give her some £3 and some of my worser gowns.

Give your father my gilt tankard and the case of silver-hafted knives, and desire him to leave them to your eldest son.
Bestow some £1 apiece of toys or black rings for my mother, my brothers and sister and their husbands and wives.

There are 4 very fine smocks in your father's little linen trunk and one of my four breadth Holland sheets for your own girl Peg.
Pay the undermaids, and poor, and Mr Aris next before the bigger sums.

Take your father's tablet picture yourself and give him Prince Henry's. They both lie in the red box, and I desire your father that he will not let any of my household linen be sold, but that it may go to you and your eldest son and I hope to his son too, only some of my broderie of my own making give to your sisters.
Now pray let none of my papers be seen; but do you burn them yourself.
All but my notes, and account and medicinable and cookery books, such keep.

Let me be buried in lead at Claydon next where your father proposes to lie himself, and let no stranger wind me, nor do not let me be stripped, but put me a clean smock over me, and let my face be hid and do you stay in the room and see me wound and laid in the first coffin, which must be wood if I do not die of any infectious disease, else I am so far from desiring it that I forbid you to come near me.

So the God of Heaven bless you all.

VERNEY PAPERS

EPITAPH ON THE MONUMENT OF SIR WILLIAM DYER AT COLMWORTH, 1641

MY dearest dust, could not thy hasty day
Afford thy drowsy patience leave to stay
One hour longer: so that we might either
Sit up, or go to bed together?
But since thy finished labor hath possest
Thy weary limbs with early rest,
Enjoy it sweetly: and thy widow bride
Shall soon repose her by thy slumbring side.
Whose business, now, is only to prepare
My nightly dress, and call to prayer:
Mine eyes wax heavy and the day grows cold.
Draw, draw ye closed curtains: and make room:
My dear, my dearest dust; I come, I come.

LADY CATHERINE DYER

PREPARING

FOR

A

FUNERAL

1666

THE hall to be hanged with a breadth of black baize
The passage into my lady's bedchamber to be hanged with a breadth of baize
The great dining room, where the better sort of mourners are to be, to be hanged with a breadth of baize.
The body to be there.
The little dining room where the ladies and gentlewomen are to be [and]
The withdrawing room to the dining room, where the close mourners are to be, to be hanged with a breadth of baize
Over the hall porch a large escutcheon on a piece of baize
That some person be appointed to conduct some of the best sort of mourners & others of chief rank into the withdrawing room, where the chief mourner and his assistant with pennon and standard-bearers are to be. That the better sort of the next mourners, and others be brought into the dining room (where the corpse is) and that the inferior sort and servants be in the hall . . . That some special servants to bring in the banquet with wine and beer.

FUNERAL DIRECTIONS FOR SIR GERVASE CLIFTON, OF CLIFTON HALL,
NOTTINGHAMSHIRE

SIR

WILLIAM

TEMPLE'S

HEART

1695

I desire my body may be interred at Westminster Abbey near those two dear pledges gone before me but with as much privacy and as small expense as my executors shall find convenient. And I desire and appoint that my heart may be interred six foot underground on the south east side of the stone dial in my little garden at Moor Park.

SIR WILLIAM TEMPLE'S WILL

Matthew Russell lying in state in the Baron's Hall, Brancepeth Castle, Durham, 1822.

... **S**IR William's house was the rendezvous of a very immoral set of men. One of his strange exploits among other frolics, was having a coffin made of copper (which one of his mines that year had produced), and placed in the midst of his great hall, and instead of his making use of it as a monitor that might have made him ashamed and terrified at his past life, and induce him to make amends in future, it was filled with punch, and he and his comrades soon made themselves incapable of *any* sort of reflection; this was *often* repeated, and hurried him on to that awful moment he had so much reason to dread.

MRS DELANY *Autobiography*

THE

DEATH

OF

BILLY.

WILLIAM

JAMES

AGED

6

DIES

AT

IGHTHAM

COURT

IN

1750

April 20.   After Dinner Dear Billy was taken with a Vomiting.

April 21.   Mr Meadhurst applied a Blister to his head . . . he was birth shaved all over his head.

April 22.   Billy is a little better. Applied 2 Blisters to his Arms about half past two in ye afternoon, clap'd Pigeons to his feet at 9 at night.

April 24.   Mr Leigh came this morning. Carried off the last of the Hop Poles. Dear Billy died at 25 mins. past 4 in ye afternoon.

April 26.   Dear Billy was Interr'd in ye Vault, was carried by four old servants . . . Mr Leigh and I went in ye coach, all ye Servants had gloves.

DIARY OF MRS ELIZABETH JAMES

ONE night, when he was in bed, a white bird, with a voice like a woman's, – or else, a female figure with a bird on her hand, – appeared to him, and told him that he must die at a particular hour on a particular night. He related the circumstances to some of his friends, who encouraged him in treating it as a delusion. The fatal night arrived. He was then at a house (Pitt Place) near Epsom; and had appointed to meet a party on the downs next morning. His friends, without his knowledge, had put back the clock. 'I shall cheat the ghost yet,' he said. On getting into bed, he sent his servant down stairs for a spoon, having to take some medicine. When the servant returned, Lord Lyttelton was a corpse.

SAMUEL ROGERS, *Table Talk*

Lord Helmsley on his death-bed, 1881.

A

DUCHESS

HAS

A

PRIVATE

FUNERAL

BELVOIR

CASTLE

DECEMBER

1825

THE Duke of Rutland left the Castle at nine o'clock for the Rev. C.R. Thoroton's, at Bottesford, there to await the coming of the funeral cortege. The nobility and gentry who had intended sending carriages, found on enquiry, that, as it was strictly considered a private funeral, the attendance of their equipages would be dispensed with.

As the Castle clock struck eleven, a signal was given from one of the towers, and the procession set out in the following order:

The superintendent of the Duke's woods, plantations and pleasure grounds, and the bailiff of her grace's extensive farm,

At the head of one hundred and thirty-six of the Duke's principal tenants of the neighbourhood, two abreast, on horseback, dressed in black, with silk hatbands and gloves.

The undertaker, on horseback.

Two mutes, on horseback, carrying staves covered with black.

Six attendants on horseback.

Two mutes carrying staves.

Plume of feathers, with the escutcheon of the deceased, borne by a person on foot

Her grace's favourite white mare, caparisoned in black, led between the two grooms who usually attended her grace when she rode out.

Her grace's coronet, on a scarlet cushion, borne by the house-steward, on a black state horse properly decorated.

THE HEARSE,

Drawn by six black horses, driven by her grace's coachman and postilion, with the family's arms richly emblazoned, and four pages on each side on foot, bearing staves tipped with silver.

Three mourning coaches and six, and four mourning coaches and four, properly decorated with feathers and escutcheons, and two attending pages in mourning on foot to each coach.

The first coach contained the Earl of Carlisle, his two brothers, the hon Wm. and Henry Howard, and Andrew Drummond Esq.

Second coach, Lord Chas. S. Manners, Lord Robt Manners, Wm. Sloane Stanley, Esq., Rd. Norman, Esq., and W.F. French, Esq.

Third coach, physician, apothecary, Solicitors, and steward.

Fourth coach, six upper men servants.

Fifth coach, six other men servants.

Sixth coach, five upper women servants.

Seventh coach, five other women servants, and nurse.

The Duke's second coachman, and two grooms as outriders, attendant upon the late Duchess' own carriage (empty), drawn by six black horses; with coachman, postillion, and two footmen.

Ten other servants of the establishment, in deep mourning on horseback.

Numerous clergymen and gentlemen of the neighbourhood.

REV. IRWIN ELLER, *History of Belvoir Castle*

Monday 30 November 1874

Blenheim Palace
12.30 p.m.   Woodstock

Dear Mrs Jerome,

    I have just time to write a line, to send by the London Dr to tell you that all has up to now thank God gone off very well with my darling Jennie. She had a fall on Tuesday walking with the shooters, & a rather imprudent & rough drive in a pony carriage brought on the pains on Saturday night. We tried to stop them, but it was no use. They went on all Sunday. Of course the Oxford physician cld not come. We telegraphed for the London man Dr Hope but he did not arrive till this morning. The country Dr is however a clever man, & the baby was safely born at 1.30 this morning after about 8 hrs labour. She suffered a good deal poor darling, but was vy plucky & had no chloroform. The boy is wonderfully pretty so everybody says dark eyes & hair & vy healthy considering its prematureness. My mother & Clementine have been everything to Jennie, & she cld not be more comfortable. We have just got a most excellent nurse & wet nurse coming down this afternoon, & please God all will go vy well with both. I telegraphed to Mr Jerome; I thought he wld like to hear. I am sure you will be delighted at this good news and dear Clara also I will write again tonight. Love to Clara.   Yrs affty

                 RANDOLPH S. C.

I hope the baby things will come with all speed. We have to borrow some from the Woodstock Solicitor's wife.

LORD RANDOLPH CHURCHILL TO MRS LEONARD JEROME

Curls of Sir Winston Churchill, aged five, preserved at Blenheim Palace.

AFTER an embarrassing inspection of my person, she [Francis Anne, Dowager Duchess of Marlborough – Consuelo's husband's grandmother] informed me that Lord Rosebery had reported favourably on me after our meeting in Madrid. She expressed great interest in our plans and made searching inquiries concerning the manner of life we intended to live, hoping, she said, to see Blenheim restored to its former glories and the prestige of the family upheld. I felt that this little lecture was intended to show me how it behoved me to behave. Then fixing her cold grey eyes upon me she continued, 'Your first duty is to have a child and it must be a son, because it would be intolerable to have that little upstart Winston become Duke.'

MEMOIRS OF CONSUELO, DUCHESS OF MARLBOROUGH

185

Ethel Buxton, aged 3 months. Drawn by her sister Ellen at Leytonstone House, Essex, 1864.

NOTES ON THE SOURCES

CHAPTER 1. ARRIVALS AND IMPRESSIONS

p. 13   H. Nicholas, *Memoirs of Sir Christopher Hatton* (London, Richard Bentley, 1847) p. 126.

p. 14   Daniel Defoe, *Tour Through Great Britain* (London, Peter Davies, 1927) II, p. 583.

6th Duke of Devonshire, *Handbook of Chatsworth and Hardwick* (London, 1844) pp. 111–12.

p. 15   William Howitt, *Visits to Remarkable Places* (London, 1840) p. 509.

p. 16   Robert Gathorne-Hardy, *Ottoline* (London, Faber and Faber, 1963) pp. 171–4.

p. 19   James Lees-Milne, *Ancestral Voices* (London, Chatto and Windus, 1975) pp. 171–2.

p. 21   Ben Jonson, *Poems* (ed. Ian Donaldson, London, Oxford University Press, 1975) pp. 87–91.

p. 23   William Camden, *Britannia* (translated Philemon Holland, 1610)

Letters of Horace Walpole (ed. Paget Toynbee, London, 1903–5) IV, p. 423

The Torrington Diaries (ed. C. Bruyn Andrews, London, Methuen, 1935) p. 30.

Journal of Princess (later Queen) Victoria, Royal Archives, Windsor.

Evelyn Waugh, *Diaries* (ed. M. Davie, London, Weidenfeld & Nicolson, 1976) p. 329.

Sacheverell Sitwell, *British Architects and Craftsmen* (London, Batsford, 1945) p. 29.

Nikolaus Pevsner, *Buildings of England: Derbyshire* (London, Penguin, 1953) p. 151.

p. 24   *Poetical Works of Alexander Pope* (Aldine Poets, London, Bell and Daldy, c. 1860) II, p. 192.

Letters of Walpole (see n. for p. 23) VIII, p. 193.

Prince Pückler-Muskau, *Tour in Germany, Holland and England* (London, 1832) IV, pp. 182–4.

p. 26   William Wordsworth, *Poems* (ed. T. Hutchinson, London, 1916) p. 477.

Constance Sitwell, *Bright Morning* (London, Jonathan Cape, 1942) p. 41.

p. 27   Henry James, *English Hours* (London, 1905) pp. 209–10.

Constance Sitwell, *Bright Morning* (op. cit.) p. 40.

p. 28   Deborah, Duchess of Devonshire, *The House: a portrait of Chatsworth* (London, Macmillan, 1982) p. 226.

CHAPTER 2. THE FAMILY

p. 31   William Howitt, *Visits* (see n. for p. 15) pp. 318–20.

p. 32   *Journal of the Furniture History Society* VII, (1971) 'The Hardwick Hall inventories', p. 32.

p. 33   F.P. and M.M. Verney (ed.), *Memoirs of the Verney Family* (London, Longmans Green, 1904) II, pp. 317–18.

p. 34   A. Jessopp (ed.), *Lives of the Norths* (London, George Bell, 1890) I, pp. 171–2.

Everard MSS, Essex County Record Office.

p. 35   *Haverfordwest and its Story* (L. Brigstocke, Haverfordwest, 1882) pp. 152–3.

p. 36   Maria Edgeworth, *Letters from England 1813–44* (ed. Christina Colvin, Oxford, Clarendon Press, 1971) pp. 162–3.

Malcolm Elwin (ed.), *The Autobiography and Journals of Benjamin Robert Haydon* (London, Macdonald, 1950) p. 417.

p. 37   Augustus J.C. Hare, *The Years with Mother* (ed. M. Barnes, London, Allen and Unwin, 1952) p. 186.

p. 38   Lees-Milne, *Ancestral Voices* (see n. for p. 19) pp. 105–6.

p. 40   E.E. Buxton, *Family Sketchbook* (ed. E.R.C. Creighton, London, Geoffrey Bles, 1964) p. 43.

p. 41   Earl of Selborne MSS.

Augusta Fane, *Chit-Chat* (London, Thornton Butterworth, 1926) pp. 46–7.

p. 42   Rosina Harrison, *Rose: My Life in Service* (London, Cassell, 1975) pp. 64–5.

p. 43   John Betjeman, *Summoned by Bells* (London, John Murray, 1960) pp. 99–101.

CHAPTER 3. GUESTS

p. 47   F.J. Furnivall (ed.), *The Babees Book*, etc. (Early English Text Society XXXII, 1868) pp. 373–4.

Historical Manuscripts Commission *Manuscripts of the Marquis of Salisbury*, (London, 1904) pp. 303–4.

p. 48   F.E. Halliday (ed.), *Richard Carew of Antony* (Andrew Melrose, London, 1953) p. 136

p. 49   *Lives of the Norths* (see n. for p. 34) III, pp. 170–1.

George Sherburn (ed.), *The Correspondence of Alexander Pope* (Oxford, Clarendon, 1956) II, p. 515

Ibid., IV, p. 185.

p. 51   Norman Ault (ed.), *Poems of Alexander Pope* VI (London, Methuen, 1964) p. 125.

p. 52   Earl of Ilchester (ed.), *Lord Hervey and his Friends* (London, John Murray, 1950) pp. 71–4.

R.E. Prothero (ed.), *Letters and Journals of Lord Byron* (London, John Murray, 1898) I, pp. 154–4.

p. 54   Pückler-Muskau, *Tour* (see n. for p. 24) III, p. 314.

John James, *Memoirs of a House Steward* (London, Bury, Holt & Co., 1949) p. 93.

p. 55   Edmund Gosse, *Life of Algernon Charles Swinburne* (London, Macmillan, 1917) pp. 95–6.

Henry James MSS, Houghton Library, Harvard University.

p. 56   Dorothy Henley, *Rosalind Howard, Countess of Carlisle* (London, Hogarth Press, 1958) pp. 42–3.

p. 57   B.E.C. Dugdale, *Arthur James Balfour* (London, Hutchinson, 1936) pp. 195–6.

Devonshire, *The House* (see n. for p. 28) p. 151.

John Jolliffe, *Raymond Asquith: Life and Letters* (London, Collins, 1980) pp. 151, 78–9.

p. 59   David Garnett, *Flowers of the Forest* (London, Chatto and Windus, 1955) pp. 108–9.

Michael Holroyd, *Lytton Strachey* (London, Heinemann, 1968) II, p. 205.

p. 60   Katherine Mansfield, *Collected Letters* (Oxford, Clarendon, 1984) p. 323.

Virginia Woolf, *Letters* (London, Hogarth Press, 1976) II, pp. 174, 197–8, 379.

Devonshire, *The House* (see n. for p. 28) p. 48.

p. 61   Evelyn Waugh, *Diaries* (ed. M. Davie, London, Weidenfeld & Nicolson, 1972) pp. 328–9.

p. 62   Harold Nicolson, *Diaries and Letters 1930–39* (London, Collins, 1966) p. 60.

CHAPTER 4. EATING AND DRINKING

p. 65   F.J. Furnivall (ed.), *The Babees Book, etc.* (Early English Text Society, XXXII, 1868) pp. 375–7.

p. 66   *The Countess of Kent's Choice Manual* (London, 1653) pp. 2, 8.

A. Macdonnel (ed.), *The Closet of Sir Kenelm Digby, Knight, opened* (London, 1910 reprint of the 1668 ed.) p. 62.

Robert May, *The Accomplisht Cook* (London, 3rd ed., 1671) pp. A7–8.

p. 69   Bradford MSS, Staffordshire County Record Office.

p. 71   Henry J. Todd, *The History of Ashridge* (London, R. Gilbert, 1823) p. 54.

Stowe MSS, Huntington Library, California.

Consuelo Vanderbilt Balsan, *The Glitter and the Gold* (London, Heinemann, 1953) p. 68.

John Evelyn, *Acetaria: a Discourse of Sallets* (London, 1699), pp. 27, 31, 69.

p. 72   P. Quennell (ed.), *The Journal of Thomas Moore 1818–1941* (London, B.T. Batsford, 1964) p. 11.

The Works in Architecture of Robert and James Adam (London, 1773–9) I, pp. 8–9.

Irvin Eller, *History of Belvoir Castle* (London, 1841) p. 329.

p. 74   Osbert Sitwell (ed.), *Two Generations* (London, Macmillan, 1940) p. 129.

Fane, *Chit-Chat* (see n. for p. 41) p. 50.

Harold Nicolson, *Small Talk* (London, Constable, 1937) pp. 75–6.

p. 78   Harold Macmillan, *Winds of Change* (London, Macmillan, 1966) pp. 188–9.

CHAPTER 5. LOVE, LUST AND MARRIAGE

p. 81   John Aubrey, *Brief Lives* (ed. A. Powell, London, Cresset Press, 1949) pp. 372, 33.

p. 82   Ibid., p. 373.

R. Latham and W. Matthews (eds.), *The Diary of Samuel Pepys* VI (London, G. Bell and Sons, 1972) pp. 158–60, 175–6.

p. 85   Samuel Rogers, *Table Talk* (London, 1887) p. 235.

Letters of Byron (see n. for p. 52) II, p. 447.

p. 86   L.E.O. Charlton (ed.), *The Recollections of a Northumbrian Lady* (London, Jonathan Cape, 1949) p. 114.

p. 88   W.H. Mallock, *Memoirs of Life and Literature* (London, Chapman and Hall, 1920) pp. 116–17.

p. 89   Nancy Mitford (ed.), *The Stanleys of Alderley* (London, Chapman and Hall, 1939) pp. 10–11.

p. 90   Scawen Blunt MSS, Fitzwilliam Museum, Cambridge.

p. 92   Anita Leslie, *Edwardians in Love* (London, Hutchinson, 1972) p. 16.

CHAPTER 6. PARTIES

p. 95   L.C. Martin (ed.), *Poetical Works of Robert Herrick* (Oxford, Clarendon Press, 1956) pp. 101–2.

p. 96   *Memoirs of the Verney Family* (see n. for p. 33) II, p. 290.

p. 97   Alice Archer Houblon, *The Houblon Family* (London, Constable, 1907) II, p. 40.

J. Greig (ed.), *Diaries of a Duchess* (London, Hodder & Stoughton, 1926) pp. 102–3.

p. 98   E.J. Climenson (ed.), *Passages from the Diary of Mrs Philip Lybbe Powys* (London, Longmans Green, 1899) pp. 185–7.

p. 100   W.J. Smith (ed.), *The Grenville Papers* (London, John Murray, 1852) II, pp. 407–8.

p. 101   Walpole, *Letters* (see n. for p. 23) VII, p. 392.

Gentleman's Magazine, April, 1801, pp. 297–8.

p. 104   Constance Sitwell, *Bright Morning* (London, Jonathan Cape, 1942) pp. 44–6.

Dorothy Henley, *Rosalind Howard Countess of Carlisle* (London, Hogarth Press, 1958) pp. 48–50, 51–2.

p. 105   Cecil Beaton, *The Wandering Years* (London, Weidenfeld and Nicolson, 1961) pp. 250–2.

CHAPTER 7. ROYAL VISITS

p. 109   Froissart, *Chronicles* (tr. Thomas Johnes, London, 1855) I, pp. 102–3.

p. 110   John Nichols (ed.), *Progresses and Public Processions of Queen Elizabeth* (London, 2nd ed., 1823) III, pp. 101–2, 110–11.

p. 112   Ibid., III, p. 91.

p. 113   Chatsworth MSS.

p. 114   Lord Herbert (ed.), *Henry, Elizabeth and George* (London, Jonathan Cape, 1939) pp. 138–9.

p. 115   Mrs Philip Lybbe Powys (see n. for p. 98) pp. 217–18.

p. 116   Robert Huish, *Memoirs of George IV* (London, 1831) I, pp. 239–40.

p. 118   MS diary of Elizabeth George, in possession of Stowe School Library, from an original communication by Philip Blackett.

p. 119   Duke of Portland, *Men, Women and Things* (London, 1937) p. 305.

p. 120   Anon [Julian Osgood Field], *Uncensored Recollections* (London, Eveleigh Nash and Grayson, 1924) p. 330.

CHAPTER 8. SERVANTS

p. 123   Furnivall, *Babees Book* (see n. for p. 65) pp. 182–3.

p. 124   British Museum, Harleian MS 6815.

p. 126   V. Sackville-West (ed.), *The Diary of Lady Anne Clifford* (London, Wm. Heinemann, 1923) pp. lvii–lxi.

p. 128   Historical Manuscripts Commission. *Manuscripts of Lord Middleton* (London, H.M.S.O., 1911) pp. 576–7.

     J.P. Cooper (ed.), *Wentworth Papers 1597–1628* (Royal Historical Society, Camden, Ser. IV, Vol. 12, 1973) p. 15.

p. 129   *Some Rules and Orders for the Government of the house of an Earle* (London, R. Triphook, 1921) pp. 44–5.

p. 130   Verney MSS, Buckinghamshire County Record Office.

p. 131   George Chandler, *Liverpool* (London, B.T. Batsford, 1967) pp. 149–50.

p. 132   Swinton Park (Cunliffe-Lister) MSS, Bradford Central Library.

p. 133   Stowe MSS, Huntington Library, California.

     A.S. Turberville, *Welbeck Abbey and its Owners* (London, Faber and Faber, 1938) II, pp. 59–60.

p. 134   Jonathan Swift, *Directions to Servants and Miscellaneous Pieces, 1733–42* (Oxford, Basil Blackwell, 1959) pp. 18–19, 24.

     Byron Letters (see n. for p. 52) II, p. 46.

p. 135   Thomas Cosnett, *The Footman's Directory* (London, 2nd ed., 1825) pp. 97–8.

p. 136   *Northumbrian Lady* (see n. for p. 86) pp. 177, 196.

     Chit-Chat (see n. for p. 41) pp. 50–1.

     James, *House-Steward* (see n. for p. 54) p. 97.

     Printed sheet preserved at Hatfield House.

p. 138   Diana Cooper, *The Rainbow Comes and Goes* (London, Rupert Hart-Davis, 1958; Century, 1984), pp. 34–6.

p. 139   Typescript memories of Gerald Horne communicated by the late David Green.

     David Freeman, *Tredegar House below Stairs* (Leaflet available at Tredegar House).

p. 140   Harrison, *Rose* (see n. for p. 42) pp. 121–2.

CHAPTER 9. ANIMALS

p. 145   John Chamberlain *Letters*

     House of an Earle (see n. for p. 129) p. 25.

     M.A. Lower (ed.), *Lives of William Cavendish, Duke of Newcastle, and of his wife, Margaret* (London, John Russell Smith, 1872) p. 58.

p. 146   Edward Lucie-Smith (ed.), *The Penguin Book of Elizabethan Verse* (Harmondsworth, Penguin, 1965) p. 152.

p. 147   B. Seeley, *A Description of Stowe* (Buckingham, 1783 ed.) pp. 8–9.

p. 149   Stowe MSS, Huntington Library, California.

     G. Eland (ed.), *Purefoy Letters 1735–1753* (London, Sidgwick and Jackson, 1931) II, p. 407.

p. 150   *Hardwick Handbook* (see n. for p. 14) p. 211.

     Boyd Alexander (ed.), *Life at Fonthill 1807–22* (London, Rupert Hart-Davis, 1957) p. 120.

CHAPTER 10. PARKS AND GARDENS

p. 153   Nichols, *Progresses* (see n. for p. 110) pp. 476–7.

p. 154   *Richard Carew of Antony* (see n. for p. 48) pp. 174–6.

p. 155   W. Lawson, *A New Orchard and Garden* (London, Cresset Press, 1927) pp. 63–5.

p. 158   Hugh MacDonald (ed.), *Poems of Andrew Marvell* (London, Routledge & Kegan Paul, 1952) pp. 89–90.

p. 159   Aubrey, *Brief Lives* (see n. for p. 81) p. 366.

p. 161   John Woolridge, *Systema Horticulturae* (London, 2nd ed., 1683) pp. 61–2.

     John Evelyn, *Kalendarium Hortense* (London, 1664) p. 63.

     John Evelyn, *Directions for the Gardiner at Sayes Court* (London, Nonesuch Press, 1932) pp. 98–101.

p. 162   Laurence Gleming and Alan Gore, *The English Garden* (London, Michael Joseph, 1979) pp. 128–9.

p. 163   Walpole at Hagley, *Walpole Letters* (see n. for p. 23) III, p. 186.

     William Chambers, *A Dissertation on Oriental Gardening* (London, 1772) pp. 5–6.

p. 164   F. Leveson Gower (ed.), *Letters of Harriet Countess Granville 1810–45* (London, Longman Green, 1894) II, p. 35.

p. 165   R. B. Beckett (ed.) *John Constable's Correspondence* (Suffolk Records Society, 1962–8) p. 98.

p. 166   Royal Archives, Windsor.

     Gertrude Jekyll, *Wood and Garden* (London, Longmans Green, 1890) p. 141.

     Nicolson, *Diaries* (see n. for p. 62) pp. 301–2.

CHAPTER 11. PLUMBING, OR THE LACK OF IT

p. 169   Furnivall, *Babees Book* (see n. for p. 65) pp. 179–80.

     Hardwick Inventory (see n. for p. 32) p. 32.

p. 170   Christopher Morris (ed.), *The Journeys of Celia Fiennes* (London, Cresset Press, 1947) p. 100.

     Philipps MSS, National Library of Wales.

p. 171   Stowe MSS, Huntington Library, California.

p. 172   R.W. Ketton-Cremer, *Felbrigg: the Story of a House* (London, Rupert Hart-Davis, 1962) p. 135.

p. 173 Ernest Hamilton, *Old Days and New* (London, Hodder and Stoughton, 1924) p. 88.
Stephen Fiske, *English Photographs* (London, 1869) pp. 196–7.
p. 174 James Lees-Milne, *Caves of Ice* (London, Chatto and Windus, 1983) p. 126.

CHAPTER 12. BIRTH AND DEATH

p. 177 J. Gardner (ed.), *The Paston Letters* (London, 1904) p. 177.
Wentworth Papers (see n. for p. 128) p. 27.

p. 178 F.P. and M.M. Verney (eds.), *Memoirs of the Verney Family* (London, Longmans Green, 1904) I, pp. 224–5.
British Museum, Add. MS 38141.
p. 181 Lady Llanover (ed.), *Autobiography and Correspondence of Mrs Delany* (1st series, London, 1861) p. 66.
Ightham Court MSS, Kent County Record Office.
p. 182 Rogers, *Table Talk* (see n. for p. 85) pp. 120–1.
p. 183 Eller, *Belvoir Castle* (see n. for p. 72) pp. 138–9.
p. 184 R.S. Churchill, *Winston S. Churchill* (London, Heinemann, 1966–) I, pp. 1–2.
p. 185 *The Glitter and the Gold* (see n. for p. 71) p. 57.

ACKNOWLEDGEMENTS

Quotations on pages 23 and 166, and illustrations on pages 56, 78, 117 and 118 are reproduced by gracious permission of Her Majesty the Queen. Thanks are due to Viscount Wimborne and Myles Thoroton Hildyard for help in getting photographs of pictures in their possession; to Frances Dimond, Peter Day and Olive Waller for assistance at the Royal Photograph Collection, Chatsworth and the *Country Life* Photographic Library; and to Clive Aslet, John Harris, Gervase Jackson-Stops, Susan Lasdun, Anne Hawker, Ann Walker, Greta Soggot, Celia Jones, Billa Harrod and Barbara Bagnall for assistance and encouragement of various kinds.

PHOTOGRAPHIC CREDITS

Endpapers (Ketteringham household: Lady Harrod). Page 1 (Baccelli servants) Lord Sackville; photo Courtauld Institute of Art. p3 (Sperlings taking tea) Neville Ollerenshaw. p5 (Manuscript) National Trust, Waddesdon Manor. p6 (View from Stowe) *Country Life.* p9 (Elveden tea party) Messrs. Sotheby's London. p10 (Blickling jug) National Trust, Blickling. p11 (Wisbech Castle) Wisbech and Fenland Museum; photo R.C. Wylie. p12 (painted screen) Victoria & Albert Museum, London. p13 (Longford Castle) Earl of Radnor. p14 (Belton House) National Trust; photo Graham Challifour. p15 (Wilton House) Earl of Pembroke. p17 (Under portico, Stowe) Buckinghamshire County Museum, Aylesbury. p20 (Newburgh priory) Captain V.W. Wombwell. p23 (Bess of Hardwick) National Trust; photo R. Wilsher. p25 (Badminton House) Duke of Beaufort; photo Royal Academy of Arts. p29 (Harden family) Abbot Hall Art Gallery, Kendal. p30 (Cave family) Lady Braye, Stanford Hall; photo Courtauld Institute of Art. p31 (Elizabeth Vernon) Duke of Buccleuch and Queensberry KT. p32 (Perseverance) National Trust. p33 (Trevelyan family) National Trust; photo Charles Waite. p35 (Catherine Allan) Abbot Hall Art Gallery, Kendal. p36 (Girl trying on garland) Victoria & Albert Museum. p37 (Blind man's buff) Victoria & Albert Museum. p38 (Capesthorne Hall) Sir Walter Bromley Davenport, Bart. p39 (Wootton House) Sir Walter Bromley Davenport, Bart. p40 (Buxtons of Northrepps) Mrs E.R.C. Creighton. p41 (Duchess of Marlborough) National Portrait Gallery, London. p42 (Lord Leconfield) Central Press Photos. p43 (Duke of Devonshire and children) Duke of Devonshire, Chatsworth; photo Macmillan. p44 (Mrs Ronald Greville) National Trust. p45 (Arthur Williams Wynn) Lady Fitzwilliam. p46 (Incident at Langton Lodge) Neville Ollerenshaw; photo Victor Gollancz. p50 (Henry Fox and friends) National Trust, Ickworth. p53 (Artist at Petworth) Tate Gallery, London. p54 (Edward Lear sketching) *Letters of Edward Lear* (ed. Lady Strachey, 1909), p173. p56 (Blenheim shooting party) Royal Photograph Collection, Windsor. p58 (Group on ice) Earl of Cawdor; photo Anthony J. Lambert. p60 (Chaplin signature) Private collection; photo Weidenfeld & Nicolson. p62 (Madresfield group) Private collection. p63 (Wilden House) photo Weidenfeld & Nicolson. p64 (Luttrell Psalter) British Museum, London. p67 ('To make a pheasant') photo Weidenfeld & Nicolson. p70 (Silhouette) Victoria & Albert Museum, London. p70 (Table of Fowl) photo Weidenfeld & Nicolson. p73 (Tea party) Collection of Mr Paul Mellon. p75 (Carved Room, Petworth) Lord Egremont. p76 (Unidentified tea-party) Royal Photograph Collection, Windsor. p78 (Sunningdale Park) Royal Photograph Collection, Windsor. p79 (Duke of Clarence) Luton Museum; photo Anthony J. Lambert. p80 (Madame Baccelli) Lord Sackville; photo Courtauld Institute of Art. p81 (Aylesford Friary) Private Collection. p82 (Nostell dolls-house) Lord St Oswald, Nostell Priory. p84 (Girl at dressing table)

The Marquess of Salisbury. p86 (Lansdownes at Bowood) Lord Newton *Lord Lansdowne: a biography* (1929). p87 (Playing the flute) Neville Ollerenshaw; photo Victor Gollancz. p89 (Bicyclists, Paddockhurst) Clive Aslet. p91 (Bootle-Wilbrahams paying court) Lord Skelmersdale; photo Anthony J. Lambert. p93 (Nelson at Fonthill) *Gentleman's Magazine*, 1801. p94 (West Wycombe party) *The Tatler*. p97 (Wynnstay theatre) photo *Country Life*. p99 (Edgcumbe party) photo *Country Life*. pp100, 103 (Festivities at Stowe) Buckinghamshire County Museum, Aylesbury, p105 (Garden party at Tredegar) Newport District Council, Tredegar House. p107 (Princesses at Cragside) National Trust; photo *Country Life*. p108 (Thomas Williams) *Country Life*. p109 (Queen Elizabeth out hunting) photo Fotomas. p111 (Elvetham) Nichols Progresses. p112 (Charles II and pineapple) National Trust. p116 (Queen Victoria at Castle Howard) *Illustrated London News*; photo Mary Evans Picture Library. p117 (Prince of Wales at Elveden) Royal Photograph Collection, Windsor. p117 (Prince of Wales, Easton Neston) Royal Photograph Collection, Windsor. p118 (Duchess of Teck, Trafford Park) Royal Photograph Collection, Windsor. p119 (Prince Henry, Lyme Park) National Trust. p119 (Duke of York, Elveden) photo Christie, Manson and Woods. p120 (Lansdownes at Bowood) Lord Newton *Lord Lansdowne: a biography* (1929). p121 (Beckford's dwarf) Duke of Hamilton and Brandon; photo Bath Public Library. p123 (Gilling musicians) photo Peter Burton. p124 (Bradford table carpet) Victoria & Albert Museum, London. p129 (Al fresco meal) photo Fotomas. p130 (Pots and pans, Erddig) National Trust. p132 (Kitchen by William Kent) Victoria & Albert Museum. p133 (Nostell dolls-house kitchen) Lord St Oswald, Nostell Priory; photo Angelo Hornak. p134, 135 (Drummond family servants) Victoria & Albert Museum. p137 (Maid at Stowe) Buckinghamshire County Museum, Aylesbury. p138, 139 (Erddig servants) National Trust; photos John Bethell. p140 (Petworth laundry) National Trust; photo Peter Jerrome. p141 (Henry Moate) University Art Collection, Hull. p142 (Van at Polesden Lacey) National Trust. p143 (Cabbage Castle) Ian Anstruther. p144 (Lord Rothschild and zebras) BBC Hulton Picture Library. p145 (Francis Russell and dogs) Marquess of Tavistock and the Trustees of the Bedford Estates. p146 (Hutton Bonville hound) Myles Thoroton Hildyard, Flintham Hall. p147 (Lord Southampton's cat) Duke of Buccleuch and Queensberry, Boughton House. p147 (Beckford dog) Duke of Hamilton and Brandon. p148 (Deer at Averham) Mr and Mrs Guy Titley; (Ledston Hall) Private Collection. p149 (Horses in stable) photo *Country Life*. p150 (Pugs at Wilton) Earl of Pembroke; photo David Robson. p151 (Formal Garden) Royal Horticultural Society. p152 (View to the Park) *Country Life*. p155 (Wilton garden) Worcester College, Oxford; photo Courtauld Institute of Art. p157 (Denham Place) Yale Center for British Art, Paul Mellon Collection. p159 (Fountain) Stephen Switzer *Hydrostaticks and Hydraulics* (1729). p160 (Enstone grotto) Plot *Natural History of Oxfordshire*. p164 (Mason's Garden, Nuneham) Private collection. p163 (Repton view) Marquess of Tavistock and the Trustees of the Bedford Estates. p164 (Sedgwick Park) *Country Life*. p165 (Stowe) Buckinghamshire County Museum, Aylesbury. p167 (Felbrigg water-closet) National Trust. p168 (Gledhow bathroom) photo Weidenfeld & Nicolson. p169 (Conduit House) The Sir John Soane Museum, London. p170 (Stowe bath) Buckinghamshire County Museum, Aylesbury. p171 (Stowe water-closets) Huntington Library, San Marino, California. p172 (Chicheley engine) Stephen Switzer *Hydrostaticks and Hydraulics* (1729); photo R.I.B.A. p175 (Elmley Castle) BBC Hulton Picture Library. p180 (Brancepeth lying in state) Viscount Boyne. p184 (Lord Helmsley) Sir Martyn Beckett, Bart. p184 (Churchill curls) Blenheim Palace. p185 (Buxton baby) Mrs E.R.C. Creighton.

COLOUR CREDITS I (Sidney family) Viscount De L'Isle VC, KG., Penshurst Place. II (Beauchamp family) Private collection. III (Sneyds at Keele) Peter Garnier; photo J.M. Kolbert, University of Keele. IV (Sir Rowland Winn) Lord St Oswald, Nostell Priory. V (Brooke family) The Marquess of Bath, Longleat House. VI (Sperlings at dinner) Neville Ollerenshaw; photo Victor Gollancz. VII (St Fagan's) Private collection; photo National Gallery of Art, Washington. VIII (Cotehele dinner) Cornwall County Library. IX (Assembly at Wanstead House) Philadelphia Museum of Art. X (Tichborne servants) Mr John Loudon. XI–XIV (Hartwell gardens) Buckinghamshire County Museum, Aylesbury. XV (Killing flies) Neville Ollerenshaw; photo Victor Gollancz. XVI (Gothic pavilion, Painswick) Private collection. XVII (Chiswick bridge) Private collection. XVIII (Unton christening) National Portrait Gallery, London. XIX (Saltonstall family) Tate Gallery, London. XX (Cholmondeley Sisters) Tate Gallery, London. XXI (Sir Thomas Aston) Manchester City Art Gallery. XXII (Duchess of Devonshire) Trustees of the Chatsworth Settlement. XXIII (Duchess of Marlborough) Duke of Marlborough, Blenheim Palace.

INDEX OF HOUSES

Figures in italics refer to black-and-white illustrations by page numbers. Roman figures refer to colour illustrations.

192